ATCHISON BLUE

"This is a generous book about an exceptionally generous community of women. Valente allows the reader to feel the warmth of Benedictine hospitality. It is a powerful thing to be accepted as we are, with all our faults and troubles, by people who are willing to listen. Valente is a good storyteller, and fortunately for us these women are willing to share their stories and insights from their daily encounters with scripture, pruning grape vines, human rights issues, the aging process and death, and the trials and joys of communal living."

Kathleen Norris
Author of *Cloister Walk*

"Seldom is 'spiritual' reading so readable as it is here! Judith Valente makes her own liminal experience in a monastery attractive, real, and profound for all of us. There will be very few who would not find her journey helpful to their own."

Richard Rohr, O.F.M.
Center for Action and Contemplation
Albuquerque, New Mexico

"In *Atchison Blue*, poet and reporter Judith Valente has created a beautiful portrait of the Sisters of Mount St. Scholastica in Kansas, and the silence, simplicity, and joy of their lives. She sharpens her descriptions by contrasting them with the demands on her own life—the anger, jealousy, and overwork that spill out as she tries to do everything expected of a modern woman.

Valente's challenges are those of all the rest of us, of course, so *Atchison Blue* becomes not only a lovely story about Benedictine sisters but an inspiring guide for everyone's struggle to find eternal silence in the midst of everyday noise."

Bob Abernathy
Anchor of Religion & Ethics News Weekly

"Many people yearn for a more contemplative life. Here is the story of a busy professional who found a way to put flesh on that yearning. In the soft light of the Atchison-blue windows and in the presence of a praying community, Judith Valente discovered the medicine of deep listening. Her story, both inspiring and humorous, has the potential to stir up the embers of your own yearning. I joyfully applaud this book."

Macrina Wiederkehr, O.S.B.
Author of *Seven Sacred Pauses*

"'Atchison blue' refers to the special color of the windows of the chapel of Mount St. Scholastica Monastery in Atchison, Kansas. Judith Valente spent many weeks with these sisters in recent years, trying to understand the Benedictine life. Usually I am not too impressed with these kinds of journalistic peeks at monastic life, finding them either too romantic or too cynical. But this account is different. Valente got to know these sisters really well by spending a long time with them. She seems to have glimpsed the inner life of this remarkable community. But Valente is more than a typical journalist. At least in this account, she opens herself to our examination, revealing aspects of her spiritual life that she finds seriously deficient. I found this account quite moving and heartily recommend it to anyone who wants to understand the spiritual life more deeply."

Terrence G. Kardong, O.S.B.
Author of *Benedict's Rule: A Translation and Commentary*

"Not only does Judith Valente capture the simple beauty and serenity of monastic life without idealizing a thing, but she also makes a powerful case for the necessity of Benedictine wisdom in our time. Compelling in its honesty, overflowing with grace, *Atchison Blue* is a marvelous addition to the spiritual writing genre made famous by Thomas Merton, Henri Nouwen, and Kathleen Norris."

Paula Huston
Author of *A Season of Mystery*

"Highly personal, yet quintessentially universal, Judith Valente's spiritual quest in *Atchison Blue* is absolutely riveting. Memorable not just for her journey, but also for how she writes of it—with the beautiful detailing of a poet and the keen exactitude of a journalist—the narrative reverberates in the mind and indelibly permeates the soul. The gentle and courageous stories she relates impart great wisdom and great joy. I felt I was in the presence of both purity and grace and could not put this book down."

Susan Hahn
Author of *The Six Granddaughters of Cecil Slaughter*

"In her spiritual memoir, *Atchison Blue*, Judith Valente does something rare. By revealing her flawed spiritual quest, she allows us to connect more deeply with our own. Nuns, silence, family feuds, and death change Valente, allowing her 'conversion of life' to whisper eternal secrets that nudge us toward our own conversations. *Atchison Blue* will uplift you, challenge you, and even make you laugh. But most of all, it may just change you."

Edward Beck
Author of *God Underneath*

"With a journalistic eye and the heart of a poet, Judith Valente leads us on a journey of exploration as she traverses the Midwestern terrain and the terrain of marriage, stepchildren, and new roles in life. It's a joy to go along for the ride."

Susan Baller-Shepard
Editor of *Spiritualbookclub.com*

JUDITH VALENTE

ATCHISON BLUE

A Search for Silence,

a Spiritual Home,

and a Living Faith

SORIN BOOKS Notre Dame, Indiana

Founded in 1865, Ave Maria Press is a ministry of the United States Province of Holy Cross.

www.avemariapress.com

Paperback: ISBN-10 1-933495-58-8, ISBN-13 978-1-933495-58-3

E-book: ISBN-10 1-933495-59-6, ISBN-13 978-1-933495-59-0

Cover image © Thinkstock.com.

Cover and text design by Brian C. Conley.

Printed and bound in the United States of America.

Library of Congress Cataloging-in-Publication Data is available.

For the sisters of Mount St. Scholastica, past and present; for all who approach the world with a Benedictine heart; and as always, for Charley.

THIS IS THE LAND WHERE YOU HAVE GIVEN ME ROOTS IN ETERNITY . . . THE GATE OF HEAVEN, THE PLACE OF PEACE, THE PLACE OF SILENCE, THE PLACE OF WRESTLING WITH THE ANGEL.

—THOMAS MERTON
The Sign of Jonas

WHEN TRUE SIMPLICITY IS GAINED
TO BOW AND TO BEND WE SHAN'T BE ASHAMED
TO TURN, TURN WILL BE OUR DELIGHT
'TIL BY TURNING, TURNING WE COME ROUND RIGHT

—OLD SHAKER HYMN

Contents

I.

Finding Light

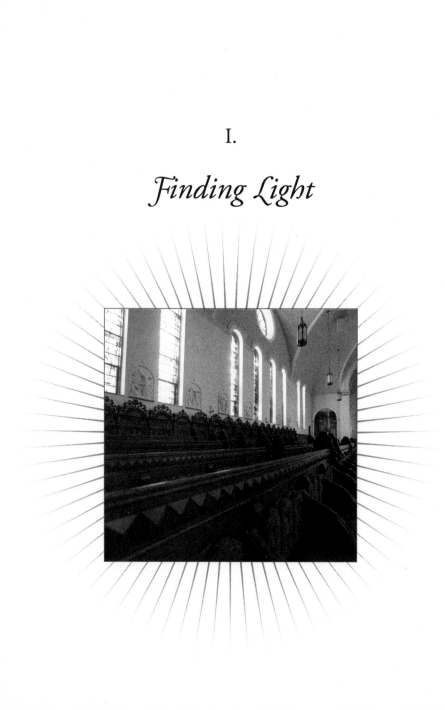

ANTHONY AND JOSEPH

One day some monks came to see Anthony of Egypt, the most renowned hermit of his day. With them was Abbot Joseph. Anthony chose a text from Scripture and beginning with the youngest monk, asked each one what it meant. Each gave his opinion as he was able. But to each one, the revered teacher said, "You have not understood it." Last of all, he said to Abbot Joseph, "How do you explain this saying?" The abbot replied, "I do not know." Then Anthony said, "Indeed Abbot Joseph has found the way. For he has said, 'I do not know.'"

—Wisdom Story
taken from *The Sayings of the Desert Fathers and Mothers*
as told by Sister Lillian Harrington, "Pilgrim Minister"

The glassmaker's art begins in simplicity. It requires only a few elemental ingredients. The artist grinds sand, soda, and lime into a fine powder. That marks the first transformation. When immersed in the crucible of fire, these three elements convert to liquid. Brushed by air, a wholly new substance emerges. Infused with color, it becomes a prism for light.

In 1947, a German-born glassmaker named Emil Frei traveled to Atchison, Kansas. He had received a commission to create a new set of stained glass windows to rise above the main chapel at Mount St. Scholastica Monastery. Frei chose a background color that merged several shades of blue. What he could not know then was that a secondary alchemy would transform his windows over time. The harsh sunlight and fierce winds of the Kansas prairie bleached the stained glass into a new color, one that today reflects a blend of sun, sky, sea, and stone. It is a distinctive gray-blue that exists nowhere else. It has come to be called "Atchison blue."

To this day, pilgrims still pray beneath the unerring gaze of Frei's blue windows. They travel to this Benedictine monastery in the heart of America's heartland, desiring transformation. Some hope to deepen an already solid faith. Some crave a temporary respite from cell phones, Facebook, Twitter, and the other white noise of the world beyond. Still others hope to repair a broken spiritual life. I have been one of those seekers.

My journey with the Mount sisters began in an oak stall in the choir chapel awash in Atchison blue. I'd come with my husband, Charles Reynard, to lead a retreat for busy professionals like ourselves seeking to slow down, find balance, and tap into the sacred. For several weekends in a row, we had dashed from city to city, speaking to various groups and working all the while at our weekday jobs—I as a religion news correspondent for PBS-TV, he as an Illinois Circuit Court judge. The morning we were to give our presentation at the Mount, I sat alone in the chapel. I wondered how I was going to speak to a retreat group later that day about nourishing the soul when I hadn't fed my own soul a decent meal in weeks.

Sunlight beamed through the stained glass, throwing patches of blue on the chapel's walls and ceiling. Silence saturated the room. I peered at the image on the window above me: St. Benedict standing with outstretched arms. Some words were written in Latin: *Omni tempore silentio debent studere.* "At all times, cultivate silence."

The paradox I had been living stared me in the face. For months, I had been talking, talking, talking, driving myself to exhaustion trying to help others live a more contemplative life. What I lacked in my own life were moments of stillness and silence when I simply could listen and *be*. Without them, I was losing drop by drop the inner reserves I needed to do my work and cultivate an interior life. In the silence of the chapel, I did something totally out of character. I wept.

I left the Mount after that first visit feeling as if something nameless had shifted inside me. I kept thinking about that moment in the chapel, the sisters I had encountered, the stories they had told. One of the first sisters I met there was ninety-year-old Sister Lillian Harrington. Something she said stayed with me. In the course of our many conversations, she often joked about her advanced age. I shared with her my own fear of growing old and dying, and I asked her if she ever thinks about death. She looked at me quizzically, then drilled her pale blue eyes into mine. "I don't think about dying," she said. "I think about living."

Living mindfully, looking beyond the obvious. I wondered if I'd arrive at my deathbed without having done either. The sisters, by contrast, seemed sure of purpose. They infused ordinary acts, such as waking, gardening, and even eating, with meaning. I sensed that monastic life had something to teach me, something I couldn't find in the self-help books lining the shelves of Barnes & Noble, assuring married, professional women like me that we could have it all. I had often returned to the writings of the Desert Fathers and Mothers, ancient Abbas and Ammas who retreated to barren settings to seek God and wisdom. But their words lacked living color. Here at the Mount were 145 modern-day Ammas, alive and well and living on the Great Plains. And yet, it wasn't as if the sisters had suddenly presented me with a neatly wrapped gift box of answers. Rather, they seemed to draw out the inner questions I had silenced.

I soon began spending an average of a week a month at the Mount. My husband joined me on weekends whenever he could. My visits to the monastery coincided with a pivotal time, both personally and professionally. It was only my second year of marriage. Although I cannot imagine a truer soulmate than my husband, I struggled as a second wife thrust into a blended family that included two adult stepdaughters who were none too happy about our marriage. I quickly discovered that the skills that served me so well as a journalist—a genuine interest in others, a can-do attitude, and a dogged determination to "get things right"—counted for little in my new role. I often joked to friends that I had become a wife, a mother, and eventually a grandmother—what takes most women a lifetime to achieve—all in the space of six months. I laughed to cover the loneliness I felt at being the outside link in my new family unit, the person who got everything wrong.

Even as I struggled to solve the divisions within my family, I felt increasingly disconnected from my church. In the public arena, so-called Christians divided the world between insiders and outcasts. Like many Catholics, I despaired over the clergy sex abuse scandal as well as the increasingly politicized statements made by our bishops—pronouncements that seemed geared at pointing to the splinters in everyone else's eyes but their own. With few exceptions, poor preaching poured from the pulpits. "The hungry sheep look up and are not fed," John Milton wrote of the Church of the seventeenth century. His observation seemed sadly accurate today. I felt myself slipping further from the faith that had been so integral to my life.

At the Mount, my husband and I experienced the vital, compassionate Church of the gospels, not a tired, passionless, and scandal-smeared bureaucracy. The sisters did as St. Francis purportedly advised: "Preach the gospel always. Use words if necessary." I once asked a retired abbot why he visited the Mount so often. He told me he found light there. "Without it," he said, "I'd be bouncing from wall to wall in a room called life, looking for the light switch."

This is the story of my journey with the Mount sisters—both the physical journeys that took me from my home in central Illinois to Atchison and the interior journey that rose and shifted within me, sometimes imperceptibly, sometimes with gale-force winds. It is a story that includes not only the sisters but also the constellation of characters that orbit a place like the Mount: the monks in the abbey down the road, the laypeople who work there, and the visitors who add their grace notes to a monastery's rhythm of life.

My early visits were mostly a time of listening and observing. Eventually, in the quiet of the monastery, I began to sense a movement of the heart, to use a favorite phrase of St. Bernard of Clairvaux. I came face-to-face with my worst demons: a quick temper; a propensity to work too hard; a tendency to be judgmental, petty, and insecure. I wrestled too with how to strike a balance between the writing work I so much loved and my desire to live a more contemplative life. And I would finally confront my long-standing fear of death, learning through the sisters to reconcile the fact of death with a love for life.

Ultimately, I would arrive at a deeper understanding of the necessities of prayer, contemplation, and silence. I would rebuild my faith within a Church that seemed increasingly withdrawn from the day-to-day realities of life. And I would grasp the meaning of two words that came to define my struggle for deep personal change: *conversatio morum*, what the Benedictines call conversion of life. *Conversatio* is like the slow, steady process that transformed the choir chapel windows into their exceptional blue color.

My sojourns at the Mount taught me something else, too. A monastery is like a mirror we hold up to the soul. It reflects back to us our weaknesses, struggles, flaws. But by looking deeply into that mirror, we can come face-to-face with an answer.

II.

Listening

STORIES

In the long, long ago, the Lord God searched for a people to be his own.

God went to the Greeks and asked, "What can you do for me if I make you my chosen people?"

"We are gifted architects. We can build beautiful temples where people can come in great numbers from all over the world to worship you."

"Thank you very much," God said, and moved on.

Then the Lord God went to the Romans and said, "What can you do for me if I make you my chosen people?"

"We are great builders of roads and bridges. We will build bridges and roads so that the people can find their way to you."

"Thank you very much," God said, and moved on.

Then God went to the Jewish people and asked, "What can you do for me if I make you my chosen people?"

An old rabbi answered for them. "We are not gifted architects. Neither are we great builders of roads and bridges. What we can do is tell stories."

And God said, "Then you will be my people."

—Wisdom Story
as told by Sister Lillian Harrington, "Pilgrim Minister"

Crossing a Bridge

To arrive at Mount St. Scholastica, you cross Contrary Creek, drive beneath God's Mountain Camp, and bypass Last Chance Road. It is a six-hour ride westward from my home in central Illinois to Atchison. First Interstate 55, then Interstate 72 slice through flat fields of corn and soybeans. Occasionally, a farmhouse or falling-down barn pops up in the distance. Aluminum grain bins glint in the sunlight. Across the Mississippi River, at the state line, the landscape changes almost instantly from flatland to hills and rolling prairies. Billboards at Hannibal, Missouri, invite travelers to visit *Mark Twain Historic Sites.* But the only site I visit in Twain's hometown on this trip is the inside of the ladies' room at the Pick-A-Dilly Quik Stop.

From Hannibal, it's a straight shot across the upper chest of Missouri to Kansas. Having grown up outside of the amusement park that's New York City, the Midwest always feels to me like the adult America—the place where you settle down to raise tomatoes and a family. This isn't exactly the Bible Belt, but it is Elmer Gantry country. *Find Jesus before it's too late!* blares a billboard near the Wooden Nickel antiques shop. Another road sign asks, *How much does an abortion cost?* Answer: *One human life.*

I have no idea how well *human* life fares in these parts, but in all my travels I have never seen so much road kill. I begin to count: four deer, six raccoons, thirteen possums. It reminds me of St. Benedict's admonition: "Day by day, remind yourself you are going to die."

Route 36 eventually curls into an old shoe of a highway, Route 59, at a town called St. Joseph. Houses with wood or aluminum siding in various stages of disrepair line the road-side. Here, the Stinkie Fingers Bait Shop offers up night crawlers and red wigglers. And the Cowboy Cobbler sits in a roadside trailer, ready to re-heel your shoes while you wait.

Closer to Atchison, the limestone bluffs over the Missouri River rise into view like a set of towering shoulders. To gaze on them is to glimpse a ten thousand-year-old part of the earth's body. A long line of coal cars from the Burlington Northern Santa Fe pauses beneath the bluffs for a rest, then starts roll-ing again with an ear-splitting wail. The BNSF is the great-grandchild of the old Atchison, Topeka & Santa Fe of song lore. Judy Garland sang of its blaring whistles, weary passen-gers, and smoking engines in the 1946 film *The Harvey Girls*. Pretty much all I knew about Atchison before I started com-ing to the Mount was that song.

I'm not expecting the set of *The Harvey Girls*, but Atchi-son is definitely not Brooklyn. A sign at the Broken Spoke Café announces, *Texas Hold 'Em every Wednesday and Friday night*. There is something broken and sad about these parts, as if time stopped ticking around 1965. Past a couple of junk-yards, gas stations, and discount liquor stores, I reach a steel two-lane bridge named for Amelia Earhart, Atchison's most famous daughter.

The Missouri–Kansas line lies smack in the middle of the bridge. I think of how many times in my life some significant event was preceded by crossing a bridge. I walked across the old Thirtieth Street Bridge in Bayonne, New Jersey, with my mother on my first day of school. I crossed the *Pont Neuf* in Paris as a college student on my way to classes at the Sorbonne.

I passed the bridges over the Thames near Fleet Street when I worked in the London bureau of the *Wall Street Journal*.

The Amelia Earhart Bridge shakes violently as a couple of semis approach from the opposite direction. Later I learn it is on the Missouri Transportation Department's list of bridges designated as "structurally deficient."

Halfway across, I spot a cross enclosed in a circle, rising from the monastery's roof. I turn left past Bradken Engineered Products—the old Atchison Casting Company—where a parade of rugged-looking men marches across the road at shift change.

Soon the monastery comes into view, its red brick wings like outstretched arms embracing the city below. My trip from Hannibal to Atchison mirrors the route taken by thirty-year-old Mother Evangelista Kremmeter, the Mount's first prioress, and the six other sisters who arrived on a chilly November night in 1863. They sought to live peacefully within a nation at war and to educate the young women of a westward-expanding land. Ever since young Mary O'Keefe (herself destined to join the monastery) saw the Mount's first home being built and called out, "The sisters are coming, the sisters are coming," Benedictine women have been an enduring presence on the Great Plains. Instead of crossing a bridge, Mother Evangelista and the others stepped off a railroad car onto a muddy path at St. Joseph, then ferried across the river to Atchison. Two carpenters from St. Benedict's Abbey (established a few years earlier) greeted them with swinging lanterns. Mother Evangelista would write later in her diary, "The love of God keeps me from fearfulness."

No men with lanterns greet me, just a twinge of trepidation. When I visited here the first time, I came as a presenter, an "expert" of sorts. Now I arrive as a seeker. I pull into the parking lot at dusk with the strong sense that my entire past has led me somehow to this monastery on a hill.

The "Work of God"

A peculiar calm accompanies the hours just before dawn. It is a wordless quiet known to the police officer returning home from a midnight shift, the schoolboy delivering morning papers, the short-order cook opening up for breakfast. And monastic men and women at prayer.

Here, Morning Praise begins at 6:30 just as light cracks open on the horizon, making early risers of even habitual night owls like myself. From the guesthouse where I am staying, I set out for the chapel. Stars light my way—the baton of Orion's Belt, the distant flare of Sirius. Morning *Praise*. More often than not, my days begin with angst, not praise—fear that I won't finish the work that awaits me or that I won't do it well enough. Smoke billows from the nearby stacks of the Midwest Grain Products plant, a giant still in the middle of Atchison, cooking up the base contents of whiskey. The roasting grain fills the air with a pleasant aroma, like bread baking.

At this time of morning, the chapel's Atchison blue windows form dark outlines. The sisters file in one by one. The younger ones sprint; the older ones lean on walkers or canes. They take their places in stalls facing one another. It is nearly impossible not to make eye contact with others in the community. At home, I have the luxury of avoiding people I find difficult: I simply freeze them out. But here, you daily face the people you live with. I imagine how hard it would be to sit across from someone with whom I've argued or just can't stand.

A candle is lit. A bell chimes. Benedictine bells, Joan Chittister writes, "call the attention of the world to the fragility of the axis on which it turns . . . Listen, *The Rule of St. Benedict* says. Listen, the bell says. Listen, monastic spirituality says." The bells ask us to listen even when we'd prefer not to.

The sisters rise and bow to one another. It is a gesture that runs so counter to our American culture, where the handshake or a hug signal instant parity. By contrast, the monastic bow says, "I humble myself before you." How different that person across the aisle looks to me when I raise my head again, having acknowledged their presence, their worth, and my own limitedness. The sisters run a thumb across their lips, make the Sign of the Cross, and sing, "Lord, open my lips and I shall proclaim your praise." These are the first words they speak each morning: a call for praise. I think of the day ahead. Can I make my actions a form of praise and not a cause for fear? Can I somehow make of this day one extended prayer?

Ever since the time of St. Benedict, the Psalms of the Old Testament have formed the heart of monastic prayer. I used to think of the Psalms as largely failed poetry. They struck me as being, by turns, whiny and mean-spirited or else saccharin and self-indulgent. They recorded a place and a time far removed from my world. But I began to view the Psalms differently during an unexpected setback in my career. I was working for the *Wall Street Journal* at a coveted assignment in the newspaper's London bureau. The year before, I had been a finalist for the Pulitzer Prize for a feature story I'd written. One morning as I showed up for work as usual, the London bureau chief called me into his office and announced that the *Journal* was having a layoff. I was among those being laid off. It was not about my work, my bureau chief told me, but strictly an economic decision.

Until that point, I believed we made our own luck. For the first time, I understood that something traumatic could happen to me that was totally beyond my control. I railed at the unfairness and questioned my talent. If I had won that Pulitzer instead of being "just" a finalist, would I have kept my job?

A Sister of Charity who had taught me in high school steered me to the Psalms. I took comfort in lines I'd previously disregarded: "Let the foot of the proud not crush me nor the hand of the wicked cast me out. . . . Do not abandon or forsake me, Oh God, my help. . . . God is for us a refuge and strength. . . . I shall see the Lord's goodness in the land of the living."

My life gradually recovered. I went on to publish two books of poetry and began a career in broadcast journalism. With each new success, my need for the Psalms seemed to fade. Seeing these prayers again, singing their words with the sisters at Morning Praise, I wonder how I could have let them go and forgotten the healing they once brought.

"One of the things that makes the Psalter so powerful is that half of the Psalms are laments," Sister Irene Nowell, the Mount's scripture scholar, told me. "And our society doesn't know how to lament. We don't want to admit we're weak, that we lack perfection."

Sister Irene asks students in her scripture classes to write Psalm-like laments based on current events. One group of students focuses on the discovery of a mass grave in Liberia. They decide to write their lament in the voice of the murderers. They imagine the killers saying to their captives, "Give to us what we could not give you. Have mercy on us."

The students turn their own struggles into songs of praise, writing alongside them the words of Psalm 136: "God is lasting love." I try the exercise myself. My stepdaughters don't accept me. *God is lasting love.* Losing my job made me feel worthless. *God is lasting love.* I am angry with my Church for driving away good people. *God is lasting love.* Praying this way reminds me my pain isn't the last word. Looking more deeply, I can find something within those trials to praise. They can become my Morning Praise.

Community prayer is also the place where the monastery and the world meet. At the Mount, Morning Praise always ends with prayers of petition. We remember the troops in Iraq and Afghanistan, as well as the people who might be killed or wounded this day by American forces. We pray for prisoners on death row, for all victims of violent crime and their families. The sisters pray for the current president of the United States, as they did for the previous one. They pray for global leaders, the sick, the dying.

I think of my husband who is at home dressing for work at this hour. He will preside today over the trial of a young man accused of sexually assaulting a college student in her apartment. The young man will say the girl invited him in for sex. A jury will be left to answer the same question posed by Pilate: "What is truth?"

I think of my oldest stepdaughter, who is probably entering her little girl's bedroom to begin their morning ritual, singing to each other, "I love you a bushel and a peck and a hug around the neck." It is *their* Morning Praise. I think of my former colleagues at the *Wall Street Journal* Chicago bureau, who will ride the elevator to the twenty-first floor and click on their computers to flesh out the news of the day. I think of the world outside—the fragile, wounded, severe, and all-too-hostile world—that has no idea a group of women is awake before dawn praying for its survival.

We will gather again three more times for prayer: at midday; at 5:30 for Evening Praise; and at twilight for Compline, the final prayers of the day. We will sing by candlelight the words that Simeon uttered when he realized he had finally seen the Savior: *Nunc dimittis, servum tuum, Domine, secundum verbum tuum in pace.* "Now, Lord, let your servant go in peace, according to your promise." The prayer permits me to put aside any misgivings I have about the day just past and any anxiety about the day to come. I am relieved of my duties; it is time to rest. Silence fills the monastery. Then we begin anew at dawn.

The monastic hours of prayer reacquaint me with the day's distinct cadences. When I worked for the *Wall Street Journal*, I'd arrive at the office at 9:00 a.m., then bury myself in work only to look out the window hours later and find it would be dark. The day had ended, and I'd missed it! Here, I go to bed with the sense of having *lived* each day. St. Benedict calls these prayer times the *opus dei*, the work of God. Can any work be more important? Morning Praise, Midday Prayer, Evening Praise, and Compline propel the Mount's rhythm of life. They begin to form the guideposts of my day.

A Conversation with Life

Dante had Virgil as his guide. St. Teresa of Avila and St. John of the Cross had each other. In one of my favorite films, *The Year of Living Dangerously*, journalist Guy Hamilton has his contemplative colleague, Billy Kwan, to shepherd him through the social underworld of 1960s Indonesia. Here at the Mount, the prioress has asked Sister Thomasita Homan to be my advisor and guide as I explore the spiritual landscape of the monastery.

Sister Thomasita, a composed, silver-haired woman, seems to radiate calmness, as if a still pond resides at her core. She once told me that as a high school student, she'd had an experience similar to mine when she looked up at the chapel's Atchison blue windows. "I suddenly realized that I never wanted to leave this place. I would never be at home anywhere else." That was more than fifty years ago.

Sister Thomasita suggests I meet with a group of Mount sisters to discuss the main threads of Benedictine spirituality and some of the questions I've come here to explore. I'm somewhat reluctant to discuss my inner struggles in the presence of a "committee." It reminds me too much of the critique panels I endured in graduate school or staff meetings where editors and reporters competed to be the most sarcastic, the most irreverent.

"Let's begin with a song," Sister Anne Shepherd, the prioress, announces. *A song? I think, What is this? Kindergarten?* Then they proceed to sing, "What can be sweeter to us than the voice of the Lord inviting us. Behold in his loving kindness, the Lord shows us the way of life. . . . " It is my first clue that monastic meetings will in no way mirror the sardonic gabfests I've experienced in the work world.

I do tell the sisters that I'm curious about how living in community changes a person. Having lived in three foreign countries and four US cities over the course of my career, I wonder too about the vow of stability Benedictines take, promising to remain at the same monastic community for a lifetime. One sister suggests I'll find answers to most of my questions by probing the meaning of two words in Latin, *conversatio morum.*

The words are as familiar to Benedictines as morning, but they are utterly new to me. I suspect they translate as something akin to "conversion of morals," whatever that means. Over dinner, I ask Sister Thomasita to tell me more. She explains that *conversatio morum* refers to a vow specific to Benedictines. Its most common translation is, "conversion of life." "*Conversatio,*" she says, "is with us day in and day out. It is only possible with careful listening and profound love—God's love and ours for one another."

I don't quite get what this means, but then she tells me something I can grasp. "*Conversatio* also applies to people outside of monastic life, whether married or single. It's a call to listen carefully, to love deeply, and to be willing to change as needed." Almost as an afterthought, she adds, "It's a constant conversation with life." I find myself returning to her afterthought even more than her definition.

Later, I look up the Latin root: "From *versatio con*, a turning with." I like the way turning connotes change because there are so many things I'd like to change about myself. I'd like to be more patient, less judgmental, more reflective. I would like to be someone who sees more than the obvious.

I sense that these two words in Latin hold the key to the kind of personal change I seek. I suspect, too, that they work on the same principle as Russian dolls. As soon as they unlock one door in the heart, it is time to step through another and then another.

"I Think about Living"

A technique that's served me well as a journalist is to explore a complex subject through the life of a single person. I thought I could better understand *conversatio* in the same way by observing how it reveals itself in the life of each Mount sister.

I arrange to spend some time with Sister Lillian Harrington, the ninety-year-old wisp of a woman I met on my first visit. The Mount sisters affectionately refer to her as one of the monastery's "icons." Her face is a well-traveled roadmap of her long life. She walks stooped over, the result of a fall she took while cooking a chicken dinner for her much-younger niece.

When I first met Sister Lillian, I confided to her that all my life I'd had a terrible fear of death. It stemmed perhaps from having parents who were middle-aged when I was born and looked more like my friends' grandparents. Grandparents had a habit of dying. As a child, I feared my parents would die too. Both ended up living long lives, but the idea of death continued to torment me. To this day, I still sometimes wake in the night gripped with anxiety that I too am going to die one day. My ninety-year-old friend exhibited no such fears. "I don't think about dying," she had said, "I think about living."

When we meet again, she tells me, "I love the possibility of each day. I probably ought to be saying, 'Lillian, you're old, and one day pretty soon you're going to die.' But I believe life is to be lived now, not in the future and certainly not in the past. As for the future, no one can predict what lies ahead. We talk about going to heaven, but we don't know the day or the hour, as St. Paul told us centuries ago. We don't really know anything about heaven either. We just believe. So all we have left is now, and I want to make the most of it."

Sister Lillian was born on a ninety-acre wheat farm outside of Blaine, Kansas, a town with a post office, a Catholic church, and a one-room schoolhouse. The youngest of six children, she was named after a sister who had died in infancy. At age sixteen, she entered the Mount community.

Hers was no Thérèse of Lisieux moment of illumination. "I didn't have a tap on the shoulder or any great sense of calling," she says. "I was on a retreat on St. Patrick's Day—terrible thing to make an Irish person go on retreat on St. Patrick's Day! A priest told me he thought I should become a sister. So I did." Years later, she learned her brother and sister thought she shouldn't have entered at such a young age. "I said, 'Why didn't you tell *me*?'"

At one point, she also had doubts. "I felt I had lost those years between the ages of sixteen and twenty-three, but then I grew out of it. What it came down to was I had made a promise, and I was going to keep my promise."

When she retired from teaching at the age of seventy, she says she prayed to discern what other work she could do. That's when her career as "The Pilgrim Minister" storyteller began. "I didn't know I was a storyteller. But people would say, 'Oh, that Lillian, she's a storyteller.' I suppose it's the way I tell a story. You have to love the story and love the people to whom you're telling the story."

I get to experience her storytelling prowess as she launches, from memory, into "Information, Please," a story about an unlikely friendship between a telephone operator and a lonely boy named Paul. When Paul accidentally hammers his thumb one morning when his parents aren't home, he reaches for the phone and dials the operator. From then on, whenever he needs help with homework, he calls the kind woman who always answers, "Information." He rings her when his songbird, Petey, dies. The operator listens patiently as he cries. "Always remember," she tells him, "there is another world to sing in."

Years pass, and Paul leaves for college. On a visit home, he decides to call his old friend. "I wonder if you have any idea how much you meant to me when I was a boy," he tells the familiar voice.

"I wonder if you know how much your calls meant to me," the operator says. "I never had any children, and I used to look forward to your calls." She tells him to ring her any-time. "Just ask for Sally."

Several months later, when Paul calls again, Sally doesn't answer.

"I'm sorry to have to tell you this," the voice on the other end says. "Sally died five weeks ago."

There is a pause. "Is your name Paul by any chance?" the operator asks.

"Yes," he responds.

"Well, Sally left a message for you. She wrote it down in case you called. Let me read it to you. It says, *Tell him I said, 'There is another world to sing in.' He'll know what I mean.*"

When I went to work at the *Washington Post*, one of the first bits of advice a female colleague gave me was, "never let them see you cry." But when Sister Lillian finishes telling the story, tears stream down my cheeks. In less than a half hour, she broke through all those years of conditioning. Perhaps it was the masterful way she relates a story that wore down those defenses. Perhaps, like the telephone operator, I don't have children of my own and wonder what impact I'll ever make on a child's life. Or perhaps Sister Lillian, so candid and unself-conscious in our talks together, gave me permission to open the curtain slightly on my own vulnerability.

"The thing about stories," she says, kind enough not to comment on my tears, "is that they can entertain, but they can also challenge. I like to say, 'All stories are true. Some even happened.'

"This story is important to me because it's about an inter-generational relationship. It reaffirms that someone my age can have an influence on younger people. The fact that tears come to the eyes of people who hear me tell it says to me that I have something to give with the stories I tell."

Sister Lillian invites me the following evening to accompany her to a presentation she will give before a group of lay spiritual directors on retreat at the Mount. Unlike me before I have to give a presentation, she doesn't seem at all anxious.

"When you get to be my age, you learn a thing or two about success and failure," she says. But she still recalls the one talk in her repertoire that fell flat. "I was just happy to be invited to this big convention and didn't really think about what I was going to do. And I flubbed up. It was absolutely terrible, just awful. Even though the man who invited me tried to tell me it was okay, I knew it was a total failure. So one thing I learned is don't go out unprepared. And I learned something else too. One speech isn't your whole life."

At the retreat center where she is speaking, she places a single sheet of typewritten notes on a desk in front of her. Then, over the course of ninety minutes, she proceeds to tell story after story from memory without flubbing a line.

Her finale is a re-imagining of the gospel story of Martha and Mary. "There's no way to know how that whole story went, so I'm going to make it up," she says to the audience's laughter. Donning one head veil and then another, she launches into the two different characters: Martha, the doer and Mary, the quiet contemplative. First, she pretends she is Martha, shopping for a meal for Jesus, and the audience members are merchants. One man offers to sell Martha beer. "Beer!" Sister Lillian exclaims. "I think Jesus would prefer wine!"

She ends her performance with a plea for balance. If you are like Martha, more comfortable being in motion, set some time aside each day to be still. "Start with five minutes and make that your sacred time. And if something professional comes up, well, for those few minutes, just bid it farewell." If you are more like Mary and have trouble getting things done, create an action plan and stick to it, she suggests. "People who are all about action might never find God. And those who are only interested in contemplation might never build the kingdom of God. Unless you mingle the Martha and Mary inside of you, you won't be a whole person," she says.

It's nearly ten at night when we return to the monastery, but Sister Lillian doesn't go to her room. Instead, she heads for the lounge in the nursing care wing where her 101-year-old sister, strapped in a reclining chair, waits for her. Mary Cummings has lived at the Mount since she was ninety-nine and suffered a debilitating stroke. Mary can barely see, but she can hear some. At night, the nurses place Mary's chair in front of a birdcage so that she can listen to the chirping of the nuthatches and parakeets inside. And every night before she goes to sleep, Sister Lillian hobbles to a small service kitchen and prepares a bedtime snack of bread, butter, and jelly for Mary. Tonight she adds a snack for me too.

Mary took a different path than her sister. She married and had six children. Back in Blaine, she had taught Sister Lillian language arts in their little country school. Tonight, Sister Lillian takes a biography of Rose Kennedy off a bookshelf. In her clear alto voice, she reads to the sister she called "Miss Mary" in grade school, until one or the other of them falls asleep.

Sister Lillian had told me, "What's important to me is that I live my life in such a way that people learn something by looking at the way I live." Her body may be stooped and frail, but a wild soul still resides in Sister Lillian. Through her, I'm learning that a passionate heart never grows old.

The World in a Single Ray of Light

For as long as I can remember, a hair-trigger temper has been just as much a part of my makeup as my eye color or love of words. Sometimes that anger is understandable, such as when my husband breaks the glass top of one of my favorite end tables five seconds after I say, "Be careful moving that table. The top is glass!" More often than not, my temper is of the lit-fuse variety. To wit, the day I vow to remain calm and patient no matter what, I blow up at the workman who is weeks behind in repairing our bathroom. My outburst doesn't make him finish the work any faster, but it does leave me angry at myself for getting angry in the first place.

I know that any real chance I have for *conversatio* will have to involve a long, hard look at why anger is such a frequent boarder in my psyche. Even as I arrived at the monastery, vowing to change, I carted behind me an unresolved conflict from my professional life that involved my field producer at PBS-TV. He and I were paired together more than ten years ago when I transitioned from print journalism to broadcast. An experienced television producer, he was sent to help me learn my new medium. As I grew in confidence—and experience—I felt he continued to treat me as if I hadn't learned a thing. He insisted on writing the scripts for my news reports, then would complain about the work. When I prerecorded the narration for my segments, he'd bark corrections at me in the studio. *He wouldn't dare treat a male colleague that way*, I thought.

The latest flare-up came two weeks before Christmas. We had begun work at 6:00 a.m. on a snowy Chicago morning. I was to record two alternate on-camera "stand ups" from memory, and we would decide later which one to use in the story. I got through the first one fine. But when the cameraman began rolling on the second, I stumbled badly. After several repeated flubs, my producer bellowed, "What's your problem? You've had those lines since last night. Didn't you look at them?"

I shot back, "If you think this is so easy, why don't you stand up here and do it yourself?" That was it. The producer told the crew to shut down.

I managed to get through the one remaining interview I had to conduct that morning, though the icy silence between my producer and me could have frozen Lake Michigan.

The next day my producer e-mailed a litany of everything he considered wrong with my work, from my writing skills to the sound of my voice. He ended by calling me "a pain in the ass." He said if I wanted to continue working for the show, I'd better find another producer.

I spent the Christmas holidays anxious and depressed, wondering if my career at PBS—and maybe even in broadcast news—was over. While the executive producer for our program assured me that I still could propose stories for the show, I would have to work with a different field producer.

My days of being handed assignments were over, at least in the short term.

When I looked back at the whole sorry incident, there were times I despised my producer. Then I'd chastise myself for having those feelings.

I have been too embarrassed to discuss my situation with the sisters. Still, I wonder how conflicts are resolved here. Surely, tempers flare in a monastery. It's a place, after all, where people with differing personalities, interests, and family backgrounds are expected to morph into a cohesive community and, under a vow of stability, stay there for life.

Sister Molly Brockwell had once spoken glowingly to me about the stability that community life offers. I decided to talk with her about what happens when matters reach a boiling point in the monastery.

If you were lost in an unfamiliar city, you would probably feel comfortable walking up to Sister Molly. She has the kind of warm eyes and inviting face strangers would approach. Though she is in her mid-forties, she looks as if she's twenty-one. Her family had moved frequently because of her father's work in the oil industry. She tells me, "My dad had a line, 'There's milk in the refrigerator, and the phone is hooked up, so we're home.'" In the Benedictine vow of stability, she found the constancy she craved. As one of her mentors once told her, stability means "we do not have to go elsewhere because everywhere is here."

And so are the problems that exist everywhere. "Living in community doesn't mean there aren't times when people don't drive you crazy or that there won't be conflict," Sister Molly begins. "There is one sister who drives me nuts! The way I do things is not the way she does things. So there may be harsh words: 'Nah, nah, nah' and all that. But in community, we can't avoid each other. Sometimes there are clear words of apology, such as 'I'm sorry I overreacted' or 'You didn't deserve that.' Sometimes it's just a matter of the next day, when she comes home from work, I'll ask, 'How did things go today?' It's a way of saying I do love you. I don't always *like* you, but I do love you. I respect you, and I value your presence."

That didn't seem on par with attacking someone's professionalism and threatening their livelihood. Had she ever experienced a more wounding conflict?

"Yes, with someone in a position of power in the community," she says. "She chewed me out in front of other people and was insensitive in other ways. It was bad. But I was blessed in that other people at the time told me this person was having some struggles emotionally. And I also had the grace to know that this was just one person. It was not the whole community. I didn't need to hang it all up."

Eventually, her feelings shifted. "It wasn't a matter of pretending something bad didn't happen. The person never apologized, but I was able to forgive her. I could not carry that anger with me for the rest of my life because I have to be here the rest of my life.

"What gets confusing sometimes is that we think liking is the same thing as respecting or loving or caring. Well, no. Liking comes and goes fast. It's a deeper relationship that says we're in this together, and there is something bigger going on between us, whether that bigger thing is our life in the community or our marriage or the business relationship we have. We can disagree with one another and not see that as a total betrayal or as a chance to hack each other to pieces or view each other as a never-ending threat."

I hear what Sister Molly is saying, but I suspect it will be a long time before I see my producer as anything less than a never-ending threat.

Sister Molly has one more story to tell me about community. When she first joined the monastery, there was an elderly, slightly befuddled sister who liked to spend time with the novices. "One day she was at table with several of us who were young, and she took my arm and said, 'Now who are *you*?' I said, 'I'm Molly. I'm a postulant.' Then she asked, 'How long have you been here?' I told her, 'Six weeks.' She smiled when I said that. She had this face that just lit up. 'You'll do fine,' she said. 'Only the nuts stay.' There's humor in that, but also what wisdom!" Sister Molly says, laughing. "We are all a little nutty. That's what makes community interesting."

There is a story in *The Dialogues of St. Gregory* about a vision St. Benedict had at the end of his life of the world suspended in a single ray of light. "That vision to me is how community all fits together," Sister Molly says. "It is really very simple when we finally realize it. Community is about the people who are sitting right next to you. It's not some lofty thing we need to aspire to. It's honoring the relationships right around us."

I think about Sister Molly's words on settling conflicts soon after they occur, about releasing anger and accepting differences. If I could muster the capacity to heed them and practice them, they might represent my first faltering steps toward *conversatio*. Still, I can't help thinking her advice makes good sense . . . in a monastery, but can it work in my world of professional pressures, big egos, and petty behavior?

A Quartet of Powerful Women

With each sister I encounter at the Mount, I seem to discover another strand of *conversatio*. When I came here seeking personal transformation, I gave little thought to how *conversatio* might spill out beyond the confines of my daily life and work. Then I met Sister Kathleen Egan.

When I walk into her room in the Mount's nursing care wing, she is seated in a wheelchair, and dressed in a crisp navy suit and a light blue blouse with a high collar. Her skin is like pale parchment. At ninety-three, she looks so fragile that I fear if I touch her, she will crumble. Yet her eyes, vivid, alert and oceanic blue, look as though they are being lit from within.

Her opening comment to me is surprisingly muscular coming from such a frail woman. "War is the greatest evil," she says. "War is demonic."

Before I learn anything else about Sister Kathleen—before I know that she is an author; the sister of the well-known peace activist Eileen Egan; and once a friend of Mother Teresa, Dorothy Day, and Thomas Merton—I learn that she is unequivocally, immovably opposed to violence in any form. It doesn't matter if it's war, capital punishment, boxing, or hunting. "Life belongs to God," she says, "not whoever has the bullet."

It's the kind of statement one rarely hears post–September 11th. Sister Kathleen's views sound somewhat naive even to a person like me, who opposed the Iraq War but saw some wisdom in toppling the Taliban in Afghanistan—using violence to curb violence, a sometime necessity.

I tell Sister Kathleen about some young men I saw recently on the news who were interviewed at what was described as an al-Qaeda training camp. They were obviously well educated and stated plainly that they hate Americans, that Americans deserve to die.

"Look more deeply into the question," she says. "Ask yourself, 'What are the needs that are putting them into that situation?' Explore the root causes of what inspires people to hate America. Address those causes."

Sister Kathleen motions for me to remove a black-and-white photograph from her bedroom wall. In the picture, her sister Eileen sits alongside Mother Teresa and a somewhat disheveled but distinctive-looking woman with large eyeglasses and pulled-back hair. Sister Kathleen tells me the third woman in the photograph is Dorothy Day.

The Egan sisters were in high school when Dorothy Day opened the first Catholic Worker House in Manhattan. "We were encouraged to go down and volunteer. I didn't do much of that, but Eileen went down right away. Dorothy said to her, 'You can come on Wednesdays and do our books.' Eileen wanted to be a total volunteer, and Dorothy asked her to do the business part—and only on Wednesdays! Not seven days a week! Eileen walked out dejected." Despite that inauspicious first meeting, Eileen and Dorothy Day became close friends and eventually traveled the world together, promoting nonviolence.

The photograph I hold in my hand was of the first meeting between Day and Mother Teresa. Eileen brought them together. "I was there at that introduction," Sister Kathleen says. "You ought to have seen those two women when they were introduced. They went to each other with their arms extended. They had the same spirit."

The meeting preserved in the photograph proved historic. Day walked Mother Teresa through the streets of New York. "I remember Mother Teresa saying, 'If I were working here with my nuns, I would open a shelter for alcoholics,' because she saw them lying on the floors of the train stations and in the streets." Not long afterward, Mother Teresa sent her Missionaries of Charity to New York. Mother Teresa eventually traveled to Atchison. "She came to see me. It was in the 1980s," Sister Kathleen says matter-of-factly, as if it was perfectly natural for a woman who had more devotees than Elvis and Jerry Garcia combined to simply drop by.

"She gave a good talk. She said, 'You Benedictines are in the right thing. You're educating the young. Don't get out of education.' She talked until about 8:30 at night. Then she asked me, 'Do you have anything to eat?' She hadn't had supper. We gave her, at that hour, sandwiches to eat."

I think about Jesus asking his disciples the same question on the road to Emmaus. At first, they didn't know it was him, though they had felt their hearts "burning." They recognized him only in the breaking of the bread. To me, it speaks volumes that Mother Teresa didn't ask sooner for something to eat. And when she did, the sisters didn't call for carryout or pop a ham in the oven right then and there. They gave her whatever they had on hand, all of them revealing their true identities in the breaking of the bread.

Mother Teresa might have been a gracious guest, but she was also an outspoken one. At one point, she suggested Sister Kathleen leave the Benedictines and join her Missionaries of Charity. "I said to her, 'Mother Teresa, I have a previous commitment.' And that shut her up. I think the Benedictine way of life is natural and full of gratitude. We see human life as a gift, one that is worthy of all our efforts to keep it a gift and not degrade it. The main message is, 'You are loved by God. No matter what happens, you are loved.' And it's great if when you leave this life, you can say, 'I loved too.'"

Sister Kathleen saw Dorothy Day one final time as well, at an evening Mass in the Catholic Worker House. By then, Day was in failing health. The altar turned out to be a wooden door set on top of a card table. Day placed a clay statue of St. Francis her sister had made next to the altar. "Dorothy said, 'Isn't this the most beautiful setting for a Mass?' A card table with a door on its side! And it was. That was one of the last times she came down from her room to have Mass."

I try to imagine that cobbled-together Mass in a dusty room at the Catholic Worker house. It probably resembled more closely the upper room of the first Eucharist than anything found in so-called consecrated churches today. I think of one of the Catholic parishes where I sometimes attend Mass in my home diocese of Peoria. It spent $8.8 million to renovate the church interior, including importing a red marble altar from Italy and commissioning three bronze statues. A cloth with gold filigree covers the altar tabernacle. It's as if the mystery of the Eucharist is a function of décor. Dorothy Day and Sister Kathleen, by contrast, understood that the heart of the Eucharistic gift lies in something so mysterious and profound, it can rise up even from an unhinged door resting on an old card table.

In the monastery's cellar is a dimly lit room that contains the personal papers of each sister. Each cardboard box is labeled in black marker with a sister's name, like the boxes the detectives pull out from storage at the beginning of every episode of *Cold Case.*

The box marked *Kathleen Egan* contains newspaper clippings of the many tributes she received as a peace activist. In one of her interviews, she lists Psalm 37 as her favorite. Not surprisingly, its message can be summed up in a few words: "settle down and be at peace." Here too are the letters she wrote to Kansas governors opposing the death penalty, the paper trail of her efforts to focus attention on world hunger, and concrete reminders of her service to Atchison's War on Poverty Council and Benedictines for Peace.

In 1995, she wrote a "to-whom-it-may-concern" letter, requesting that upon her death, her eyes and body be donated to the University of Kansas Medical Center and any money left from her book royalties be donated to the poor.

I think about the constancy of Sister Kathleen's commitment to nonviolence and her concern for the poor. I think about how that commitment springs not from a set of political beliefs but from living a principled life. Her faith expressed in the real world of war and peace, haves and have-nots transcends politics.

As much as I hope for *conversatio* in my own life and am learning more about it from Sister Kathleen, I'm beginning to see that personal transformation counts for little if it does not extend outward. Thomas Merton spoke of the need for contemplation and action. Like Sister Lillian, retelling the story of Martha and Mary, he pointed out that contemplation alone doesn't feed the hungry, teach the uneducated, clothe the poor, or stop the violence. "We must work together as Americans and Christians, as brothers and builders," he wrote toward the end of his life. "I, with my books and prayers, you, with your work and prayers. Separately we are incomplete. Together we are strong with the strength of God." Sister Kathleen and Sister Lillian recognized that long ago.

A Leaving

I am to return home tomorrow after spending my first two-week visit at the Mount. I wonder if I'll embarrass myself by breaking down in tears publicly when saying goodbye. It almost happened this morning at Morning Praise as I listened to the voices singing as one and watched the sisters file up for Communion in their plain, hand-me-down clothes from their secondhand shop. I recognized this feeling. It's the same one I would experience after a visit to my parents whenever I had to say goodbye to return to my work at the *Washington Post* or the *Wall Street Journal*. It felt like being ripped from a cone of protection and thrown again into an arena where I often felt uncertain and inadequate. Eventually I'd regain my equilibrium, but the partings never got easier.

My last evening coincided with the annual employee picnic, a party the sisters throw on their front lawn for the workers who mow the grounds, help with the laundry, cook in the kitchen, and care for the sisters in the monastery's assisted living wing. Employees bring their spouses, children, and grandkids. Everyone sits on lawn chairs and eats hamburgers, hot dogs, potato salad, and ice cream sundaes until the sun goes down. That night, I met Big Pete and his son Little Pete, who is actually a gargantuan man with a shaved head. Both received awards for their years of service.

At sunset, the sisters stood and, with extended arms, sang a blessing over the workers: "May the Lord look upon you with kindness. May the Lord fill your heart with holy peace. God's love be forever within you. May the Lord always bless you and keep you." Most of the employees, Big Pete and Little Pete included, had tears in their eyes.

A few days earlier, Sister Anne, the prioress, blessed a new garden just outside the monastery's assisted living wing, where the elderly sisters plant roses and coleus and cultivate small plots of tomatoes. Sister Anne said Benedictines have always cultivated gardens. Gardens remind the world of the need for beauty. Then, one by one, she sprinkled each flower bed, bush, and plant with holy water. Lastly, she blessed every person in attendance.

I thought of how attentively even seemingly ordinary acts like planting a garden are celebrated here and mined for their deeper meaning. I wonder why my husband and I don't bless our little flower and vegetable garden at home with our friend Linda Benedict, who helps with the planting each year. We should have blessed our house this summer when we repainted the bedrooms and hallways. We should have blessed the painters and Linda, the gardener, too.

The sisters voted to name the site "Mary's Garden" in honor of the Virgin Mary and Sister Mary Agnes Patterson's mother (whose name was Jean, but that was beside the point). Sister Mary Agnes and her mother had spent many hours clearing the plot of land. Jean Patterson didn't live to see the garden take root, but at the blessing, her daughter noted how she was probably rejoicing over it in her new life.

The simple beauty of the blessing ceremony, the remembrance of mothers gone, and the thought of having to leave the Mount wrenched the emotions I had been trying to keep in check. I started to cry right there over the black-eyed Susans. One of the sisters put her arms around me and asked if I was all right. I was more than all right.

"We Are All a Little Nutty"

Several weeks have passed since my first extended visit to the Mount, eroding the sense of balance I had drawn from the community and its prayer life. I feel as if I am again drowning in an undertow of work and personal commitments.

Before I left for the Mount, I'd sent a story proposal to my executive producer at PBS, suggesting we profile the concert violinist Rachel Barton Pine. By the age of twenty, Pine was on the verge of a spectacular performing and recording career.

A tragic accident in 1995 changed all that. She stumbled as she stepped out of a commuter train in the Chicago suburbs and was dragged for several feet along the tracks. Caught under the churning wheels, one leg was severed, the other badly mangled.

After forty surgeries and years of rehabilitation, Pine could walk with the help of prostheses, and she had begun performing again. She credited her faith with helping her heal emotionally and physically.

When I open my e-mail one morning, I'm stunned to see a message from my former field producer. We have not spoken for several months. His message is semiconciliatory. *I would like to work with you on the Rachel Barton profile*, it said. *We have had our differences, but this is the kind of story we've worked on and done well in the past.* Though not an apology, the note, nevertheless, cracks open a door.

Nervous and determined to be well prepared, I repeatedly practice my on-camera stand up before I have to record it outside Pine's childhood church in Chicago. On my first try, I give a flawless delivery. We do a second take just for safety. The rest of the videotaping goes smoothly. I suppose the privilege of observing so closely the artistry of such a talented musician has filled our entire crew, my producer included, with a sense of awe and gratitude.

In a break between taping, I take a long look at my producer. He is a man hastening to the end of his career—a career that, by his own admission, he often put ahead of his personal life. I am certain he knows this PBS job will probably be his last full-time job in the business. He may wonder what the rest of his years will be like without the professional work that's given his life context and meaning. He behaved badly the last time we worked together. So did I.

The Mount sisters used to observe a tradition whenever two or more teamed up to work on a project. They would bow to one another and say, "Have patience with me." I think of how much more pleasant my work might be if, at the start of an assignment, I bowed to my colleagues and they to me, and we asked one another for patience with our failings. "We are all a little nutty," Sister Molly had said when I inquired about how conflicts get resolved in the monastery. I remembered something else she had said. People can disagree and not see it as a total betrayal. We don't have to view the other person as an eternal threat. As she put it, "Life goes on."

With the Rachel Barton Pine profile, my producer and I managed to collaborate peaceably. We were able to broadcast the story of an exceptional musician who had overcome a seemingly insurmountable setback. For all three of us, life goes on.

"I'm with You in Your Sadness"

We sometimes receive the most momentous news in the most prosaic of places. On the morning that my father dies, I am waiting in line in the optical department of Sam's Club. My cell phone rings as the other shoppers whiz by with their overloaded carts. It is my sister calling from Mobile, Alabama. She wants to let me know that my ninety-seven-year-old father has had a rough night and needs to see a doctor. My brother-in-law found him dazed and seated on the bathroom floor. My father has always been a taciturn man given to understatement. When my brother-in-law asked him what he was doing on the floor, my father said he was simply trying to get up.

My sister asks if I would like to speak to my father. I hear the stairs creak beneath her as she climbs to his bedroom. She calls out, "Dad, Judy's on the phone!" Then she pauses. After several seconds, she whispers, "He's dead."

"Don't kid around like that," I snap back.

But she was not joking. My father lay with one eye closed, the other eye staring cross-eyed at the ceiling. He wasn't breathing. I told my sister to hang up and call 9-1-1. For twenty minutes, I nursed the fantasy that somehow my sister was in error, that the paramedics would miraculously revive him.

The call confirming his death soon followed. At some point, he apparently laid down and never woke up, his fresh clothes for the day—plaid shirt, tan sweater vest and corduroy slacks—still spread out beside him. The death certificate would list cause of death as "multiple infirmities of the aged."

Given his advanced age, my father's death was intellectually no surprise. And yet it was stunning. Just two weeks before, my husband had accompanied my father back to my sister's home after one of his extended visits with us. He looked better than he had in a long time. "We'll see you at Thanksgiving," I'd said when we parted at the airport. And for once, the thought didn't cross my mind that this might be the last time I saw him alive.

The first person I want to call with the news isn't a family member. It's Sister Thomasita at the Mount. She had once told me about the day her father died. Richard Homan Sr. had grown steadily weaker in an intensive care unit. Occasionally, he would struggle to speak some words of encouragement to his family. One day, he startled both his family and the medical staff: He removed his oxygen mask and began singing. The song was "Ain't She Sweet," a favorite of his wife Veronica, who had died two months earlier. When he finished the song, he looked up and whispered, "Veronica, please meet me halfway." Then he lifted his head from the pillow and kissed the air.

"Mom was apparently right there because Dad sustained that kiss for a long time," Sister Thomasita recalled. He died moments later.

I suppose, in calling Sister Thomasita, I'm looking for someone who believes death isn't the end of life, but merely a case of "moved elsewhere." I can't get her on the first try but am put through to Sister Mary Agnes, the Mount's former prioress. She assures me the sisters will pray for my father by name at Evening Praise. That comforts me. I've already argued with the pastoral care minister at the church where my father will be buried. I want to be able to read a poem I've written about him at the funeral Mass, as I did for my mother at her funeral seven years before.

The pastoral care minister informs me, "Monsignor doesn't allow that. It's against canon law."

"Canon law is nonsense, and you can tell that to the Monsignor," I shoot back.

What I really mean to say is that the priest who is to preside at the funeral never met my father. How can he speak about the man who kept a blue rubber band wrapped around his ring finger where other men wore a wedding band; who collected odd things, such as empty Quaker Oatmeal packets, the tin tops of coffee cans, or the string from tea bags, saying, "These things could come in handy"; and who could fashion a snow shovel out of an old broomstick and a discarded license plate? And though he surely never read Tennessee Williams, once clipped a photo of ice-covered trees from the newspaper, titled it *The Glass Menagerie*, and tacked it to our cellar wall. Who would tell these stories?

Sister Thomasita calls a short time later, and I am relieved to hear her calming voice. I may not be allowed to recall these memories for the mourners at my father's funeral Mass, but I can tell them to her, and I know she will listen with the ear of her heart. She doesn't stretch for facile things to say, such as "He lived a good long life," "He went peacefully," or "He's with God." She says simply, "I'm with you in your sadness."

———————————— ✄ ————————————

Within days, handwritten notes begin arriving from the Mount sisters. The prioress writes to say a Mass will be said in honor of my father. Sister Lillian sends a poem she has written. Years before, when my mother died suddenly of a stroke, I felt completely adrift in my grief. My older sister and brother were ensconced in their own sadness. My then-fiancé (not my wonderful current husband!) seemed enraged that my mother's death had taken my focus off of him. With my father's passing, I feel as if I have the support of 145 Mount sisters grounding me from afar. I take comfort in knowing the sisters are praying at the end of the day for those who have died and those who grieve. I think of the words of Psalm 33: "The Lord looks on those who hope in his love to rescue their souls from death."

Even with that comfort, my father's passing intensifies my fear that there is nothing beyond this life. I once interviewed the executive director of the Freedom from Religion Foundation. She called belief in an afterlife "a fine fiction" humans have created to deal with the terror of their own demise. "Death gives life its meaning," she said. "If life went on forever, it would no longer be as precious." I remember questioning that then, and I question it again now. Why can't we go on in perpetuity? We could become like Yoda in *Star Wars*, gaining wisdom all the while, dispensing koan-like truisms to younger generations, such as, "Do or do not. There is no try." And yet, even Yoda seems to accept the fact of death. "Rejoice for those around you who transform into the Force," he tells Luke Skywalker. "Mourn them, do not."

What I remember most vividly about my father's funeral is the body in the casket. He was one of the least excitable people I have ever known, yet the morticians managed to press his lips into a frown. How *empty* that body seemed. As an old man, my father grew more sensitive to the cold and often walked around the house with an extra shirt thrown over his shoulders, even in summer. I think of how cold he must be now beneath the hard, silent earth. I picture the Mount sisters singing the *Nunc Dimittis* at twilight, praying the words of another old man: "Now, Lord, let your servant go in peace, according to your promise." I imagine those prayers as a cover for my father against the cold.

III.

The Movement of the Heart

The Trouble with Epiphanies

Christ came into my room
and stood there,
but I had work to do.
I didn't ask him to sit down;
he would have stayed all day.
I said to him after a while,
"So what do you want?"
He laughed and said
he was just passing by
and thought he'd say hello.
"Great," I said, "hello!"
And so he left.
But I was so damned mad by then
I couldn't even work,
so I went and got some coffee.
The trouble with Christ is
he always comes at the wrong time.

—Wisdom Story
attributed to John L'Heureux
as told by Sister Lillian Harrington, "Pilgrim Minister"

In the Presence of Gratitude

When I return to the Mount in mid-December, the memory of my father's death is still a throbbing wound. "You must come the third week of Advent," Sister Thomasita tells me. "The prayers are so hopeful then." Hope is a therapy I could use.

I arrive just after a heavy snow and in time for the going-away party for Sisters Presentasia and Susana from Tanzania. The African sisters lived at the Mount while completing their college degrees. In a few days, they will return home. The sisters have raised a sign in Swahili that says *Hongera Mungu Akubariki.* "Congratulations, God bless you."

This will be a night of storytelling. Sister Mary Agnes, the Mount's former prioress, recalls accompanying Sisters Presentasia and Susana from the airport to the monastery. On their first night, they knelt on the floor and thanked the Mount community for providing them an education. "To live with the African sisters," Sister Mary Agnes says, "is like being in the presence of gratitude all the time."

I picture those sisters kneeling before their peers. How counterintuitive the gesture seems in our American culture. But why not, once in a while, kneel before others to show our gratitude for their presence in our lives? In my own life, the person I would start with is my husband.

Sisters Presentasia and Susana beat conga drums and lead the community in a hip-swinging African hymn called "*Ee Bwana, Mimi Nitakusifu*" ("Oh Lord, I Will Praise You"). The Mount sisters join in, playing castanets, maracas, and cymbals that have been placed at each table. Even the seventy-year-olds sway to the pulsing beat. I think about how leisure is just as much a Benedictine value as prayer, community, listening, and hospitality.

Coincidentally, the next morning's gospel reading is the familiar story of the Annunciation, the angel Gabriel's visit to Mary announcing the coming birth of the Christ Child. I've often wondered how Mary remains so sanguine. Though she witnesses earth-shattering events, she seems to barely lift an eyebrow. Sometimes I wish Mary would show a little more fight. I want her to talk back to the angel and say, "Give me a break!" I want her to get angry at Joseph for taking her on a trip when she's nine months pregnant and then not planning ahead for lodging. I'd even argue that on the afternoon of the Crucifixion, she would have been within her rights to express what St. Benedict calls "the wicked zeal of bitterness," maybe establishing a protest group such as MACC (Mothers Against Criminal Crucifixion). Instead, we read about a woman who ponders the incomprehensible in her heart, who says, "I am the handmaid of the Lord. . . . May it be done to me according to your will." It would hardly have been my reaction.

But what strikes me most in hearing this familiar gospel once again is that the angel doesn't come when Mary is cooking or washing clothes or working in the fields or even praying. He comes when she is apparently doing nothing in particular. She's at leisure.

Leisure wasn't always a word in my vocabulary. When I worked for the *Washington Post*, one of the top editors complained that reporters were leaving the office at 6:30 at night. I suppose he thought we should stay until midnight. He held up as a model one of my colleagues, a chain-smoker in his twenties who always looked in need of a good meal, and remained at his desk late into the night and on weekends. When I went to work for the *Wall Street Journal*, reporters used to joke that the mantra coming from the *Journal's* New York office was "more, more, better, better." By contrast, the Benedictines might argue that as a culture, we suffer from leisure deficit disorder.

Whenever I'm driving myself too hard, it's an easy leap for me to fall into "the wicked zeal of bitterness." I'm harder to live with. I lose my temper more quickly. I have to remind myself of a friend who likes to quote the White Rabbit in *The Adventures of Alice in Wonderland*: "Don't just do something, stand there!"

The Benedictine motto, *Ora et Labora (Pray and Work)*, is a plea for balance. Early on, the Mount sisters tried to teach me there's a right time and wrong time for both. One evening around eight, Sister Anne, the prioress, saw a light on in my room. I was still writing away on my computer. She knocked on the door and invited me to shut down the computer and join her and some visiting prioresses for a beer. Stupidly, I chose to keep on working.

The Mount sisters work, pray, and play with equal gusto—as they did at the party for the African sisters. It's a way of saying leisure, too, is holy. If given the chance again to turn off the computer and raise a glass with friends, I'd probably do it. I don't have to work constantly to prove my worth. As one of the sisters told me, "Sometimes it's enough just to live your life and love the people you love." Or even just stand there.

A Child's Birth, a Young Man's Death

As liturgical seasons go, Advent reminds me of the cool-down period after a workout. It's a time to dial back the exercise, take stock in what has or hasn't been accomplished, and set some new goals.

In the Advent readings, poetry, hope, and promise abound. "Raise a glad cry, you barren one who did not bear, break forth in jubilant song," the prophet Isaiah exclaims. "I will save the lame and assemble the outcasts," says Zephaniah. And from Chronicles: "For you have made a promise regarding your servant's family reaching into the distant future." Sometimes the readings make me feel downright giddy.

As a childless woman, I especially love the women of Advent—all those surprise pregnancies. There is Manoah's wife (her name isn't given) in the book of Judges, who was thought to be barren. Not! Then we have Elizabeth and Zechariah, who become parents "in their advanced age." And of course, Mary's unlikely pregnancy. As Henri Nouwen once said of monastic prayer in Advent, "The songs, lessons, commentaries and antiphons all compete in their attempt to set the stage for the Lord who is to come."

The comfort I get from the daily readings soon begins to fade. Perhaps it was too ideal to last. A few days before Christmas, the sisters receive word that a twenty-year-old student from Benedictine College, the college they cosponsor in Atchison, has died in a tragic accident. His name is John Paul Forget. Though the family pronounces the name as *For-jay*, I can't help but think of the irony carried within the English pronunciation.

The accident happened on the snowy night the sisters celebrated with Sister Presentasia and Sister Susana. John and four other students, three women and the young man who was driving, were headed home for Christmas break. Traveling on Interstate 70, their car hit black ice on Boone's Bridge over the Missouri River. The vehicle swerved and spiraled into donuts. The women screamed. John Paul called out, "Lord, help us."

The car finally came to rest against a concrete barrier on the right side of the bridge. Its headlights were smashed, and the engine wouldn't turn over. The students sat silently for a few seconds, shaken but unhurt. Through the rearview mirror, they could see a semi barreling toward them in the swirling snow.

"It's going to hit us!" John shouted. The women jumped out of the car and plastered themselves against the concrete barrier. John Paul and the driver hopped over the barrier and held on, balancing their feet on a metal beam beneath the bridge. The semi barely missed their car. No one is sure what happened next, except that a voice called from the water, "Help! I'm down here!" But in the darkness and blowing snow, they could see no one. They realized John Paul had fallen into the icy, pitch-black river. Eventually, there was silence.

Police arrived, but, because of the ice, couldn't send a search boat into the river. They used a spotlight to scan the water. But John Paul was gone.

It's now been three days since the accident. John Paul's body still hasn't been found. The family has decided to call off the search. Details about John Paul, "J. P." as his friends called him, trickle into the monastery. He was the oldest of thirteen children. Named after the late pope, he entered seminary for the priesthood but left to continue his studies at Benedictine College. He went to Mass daily. I can't help but think, *Why this boy? How can anyone reconcile this tragedy with the God of hope reflected in the Advent readings?*

News of John Paul's death arrives the day before I'm scheduled to spend time with Sister Chris Kean, who works as a funeral director. The story of Mary Magdalene and the others who rushed to Jesus' tomb inspired this soft-spoken woman of few words to enter her line of work. "They were going to the tomb to preserve his body, but they were doing something else too," she says. "They were ministering to one another in their grief."

Sister Chris calls it "a privilege" to be with the dead and "look into the face of somebody who has just seen the face of God." As an undertaker, she has prepared the bodies of children and babies who died, as well as the bodies of murder victims. I ask her how, as a woman of faith, she accounts for tragedies like murder, and the deaths of children and a promising young man like John Paul.

"We're all here for an appointed time," Sister Chris says slowly, choosing her words. "And for some of us, that time is shorter. There are some people who do their work on earth quickly. And once that work is done, they go on to their reward. There is no more reason to be here. In John Paul's circumstance, he had been in seminary. He was trying to discern if his life was going to be given over to God. Maybe this was God's way of saying, 'It's okay. You've done fine. Come home.' What is it, after all, that we're hoping for at Christmas? We're hoping for the birth of Christ, yes, but we're really hoping for a Redeemer. John Paul has already gotten that. So what we're mourning now is *our* loss."

I grasp these words intellectually but find them hardly comforting. I'm more in line with Sister Lillian, who admits we don't *know* if there's life after this one. We just believe it.

The monastery prays for John Paul and his family at community prayers over the next several days. I'm struck by how the daily rhythm of life continues unchanged. The sisters bake cookies and make jellies to give as gifts. Christmas cards get hung on a wall. When I question Sister Thomasita about this, she says, "People react to something as tragic as John Paul's death knowing that God's unconditional love cannot be outdone. We don't always know what that means, especially when it comes clothed in mystery as dark as this young man's death. But we live with trust and faith. That allows us to go on with the things of our daily lives, though we may be doing them, as Emily Dickinson writes in one of her poems, 'in a wooden way.'"

Throughout Advent I've been reading Nouwen's *The Genesee Diary*, about his sojourn at a Trappist monastery in upstate New York. I discover a passage that makes a great deal of sense now: "A monastery is not built to solve problems but to praise the Lord in the midst of them."

The truth is, there aren't any answers to explain this young man's death in the way journalists like me—and much of the world—expect and demand answers. It's why perhaps I find myself drawn more and more each day to the hope-filled readings of Advent, where the thirsty find water, barren women give birth, and outcasts are welcomed. Today at Mass we sing, "From every foe deliver them that trust your mighty power to save and give them victory o'er the grave." Words that seem meant for John Paul Forget, whom we do not forget.

"Christified"

Every Christmas season, the sisters set out through a door marked Pax to deliver cookies and meals to "friends of the monastery." They dole out the cookies—two thousand in all—on colored plates wrapped in cellophane and topped with a typewritten sticker that says *Merry Christmas from the Benedictine Sisters*. One of our first stops is the home of Julie Haggerty, who cut the sisters' hair for years and is now suffering from bone cancer. When we arrive, Julie is lying on her couch, just back from a bone marrow treatment. She is pale, emaciated, and barely able to speak. "My wife probably received two hundred cards this Christmas," Julie's husband says. "The only ones she'll look at are from the sisters."

On Christmas Eve, with the temperature wavering between zero and two degrees, a group of us again head out, this time to pick up boxed dinners of turkey, mashed potatoes, and string beans for delivery to shut-ins. We drive through parts of Atchison not included in the visitor brochures touting the town's picturesque bluffs, Missouri River walk, and restored Victorian homes. Sister Thomasita and I form part of the delivery team for residents at Santa Fe House, a complex for senior citizens. We knock on the doors of two elderly women, who receive their meals with gracious, if somewhat embarrassed thanks. I wonder if they have no children or grandchildren to visit them. The dimly lit hallways, the pathetic-looking garland from Wal-Mart strung across the walls, and the thought of these women alone on Christmas Eve makes me want to cry.

We inch our way across a thick pillow of snow to our next stop, a house that looks as if Freddy Krueger might live there. Sister Mary Agnes, who is on our delivery team, decides to ring the doorbell alone in case the porch won't support both our slender frames. Empty beer bottles litter the front lawn. I begin reflexively picking up the trash to toss in the garbage, but then Sister Mary Agnes hollers from the porch, "Don't touch that stuff!" She hands over the meal to a husky young man who comes to the door. He takes the food without uttering a word. I wonder if the elderly woman it was meant for will ever eat a morsel of that turkey.

As we ease our way back to the monastery on snow-coated streets, I think of the hoopla over Black Friday and Cyber Monday shopping, of the football field of "gifts for under $10" on sale at Atchison's Wal-Mart, which will likely end up tossed in a closet or gathering dust on a shelf. They make these homemade cookies and boxed-up meals seem all the more like treasure. The sisters don't personally know most of the "friends" who receive their gifts. They simply hear of a need and respond to it. *Yes, that's it*, I think. *That's what Christmas should be: giving to the stranger.*

I could talk here about how beautiful the Mount's crèche looked awash in blue and white Christmas lights, how sunlight bathed the choir chapel's Atchison blue windows, or how we sang a round of *Jubilate Deo, omnis terra, servite domino in laetitia!* "Everyone in the land, rejoice, serve the Lord with gladness!" as we sat down to dinner. But what I will remember most about my first Christmas at the Mount is Sister Anne, the prioress, standing before the community to give her annual "Christmas Message." And it was this: to ask the forgiveness of any members of the community she may have hurt in any way during the course of the year.

Then, Sister Mary Elizabeth Schweiger, the subprioress, speaking on behalf of the community, told Sister Anne, "If any of us have hurt you in any way, we ask *your* forgiveness."

In this way, they go forward into each new year with the slate wiped clean of the past year's messes. In her Christmas Eve reflection, Sister Anne quotes the English Benedictine Maria Boulding:

> "If you are at times so weary and so involved in the struggle of living that you have no strength even to want God, yet are still dissatisfied that you don't, you are already keeping Advent in your life.
>
> "If you have ever had an obscure intuition that the truth of things is better, greater, more wonderful than you deserve or desire . . . or you could ever suspect, you have already been drawn into the central mystery of salvation. For Christ is born in us continually as our minds, our actions, our reactions, our relationships, our experiences and our prayers are *Christified.*"

This Christmas, I didn't write a single card. I haven't even mailed out the small presents I bought for family and friends from the monastery's gift shop. In stripping away all the usual trimmings of Christmas, I experienced something far more mysterious and unforgettable: the intuition that Christmas *is* better, greater, more wonderful than I had ever imagined.

After celebrating his first Christmas at the Abbey of Gethsemani, Thomas Merton wrote in his journal, "You who are in the world: let me tell you that there is no comparing these two kinds of Christmas. . . . It is good to know that somewhere in the world there are men who realize that Christ is born." And continually here at the Mount, women too.

Families

Being a stepmother, or "step" anything, is one of those jobs you wish you could contract out. Although it is a first marriage for me, my husband has two adult daughters from his previous marriage. Though their parents have been divorced for years, both my stepdaughters still struggle with the decision. I entered this picture with an idealized notion of what it would be like to have stepchildren—each of us learning to take steps alongside the other in our new family unit. I never imagined how gingerly I'd have to trod.

Ours was not a mad dash to the altar. Charley and I knew each other as "poetry friends," people who ran into each other occasionally at poetry readings. We didn't go on an actual date until his divorce was final. Then we dated for nearly three years before getting married. Still, my younger stepdaughter—twenty-two years old at the time—burst into tears when we announced our wedding plans. She said it was "too soon."

A routine family get-together can become a tinderbox of tensions. Add to the mix the emotional strain of the holidays—when hardly anyone's expectations of what *should* be are met—and the tinderbox can turn into a conflagration.

The first Christmas after we were married, my husband and I arrived at my older stepdaughter's house with an armful of gifts. She ended up putting me out of her house within the first hour. She accused me of endangering her newborn because I was getting over a cold. I hadn't even been in the same room as the baby. The real message, I suspected, was that both my stepdaughters considered me toxic to their family dynamic.

Ever since then, the prospect of a holiday visit with my husband's daughters fills me with a monumental sense of dread. After spending my first Christmas at the Mount, and with a running case of anxiety, my husband and I set out to visit my older stepdaughter and her family. We pack up our gifts as well as some pasta we picked up for her on a vacation in Italy. We think she will enjoy it because she studied in Italy as a college student. I've also bought some vegetables I think she'll like from Nick, our favorite Greek wholesale grocer in Chicago. When we tell my stepdaughter over the phone about the pasta and vegetables, she tells us not to bother bringing them. She and her family eat only organic foods.

Again, I feel as if I am always several steps out of sync with my stepdaughters. We manage to spend a weekend together without any flare-ups, but I feel as if I am in the home of strangers. I wonder how it is I can feel so disconnected to people who are a part of the man I love more than anyone in the world. As another year ends, I feel increasingly hopeless that our family will ever be blended, or ever be family. Though I'm grateful to be part of another family now—the community of the Mount—I also know that any chance I have at living *conversatio* will mean confronting the dysfunction in my own living room. Finding a way through that struggle weighs heavily on me as I await my next visit to the Mount.

Silence

The moments I love best at the Mount are the times when I can wander the corridors alone, in silence. I breathe in the monastery's strong, clean scent, a mixture of wood, incense, and candle wax. The scent of peace.

The Rule of St. Benedict overflows with praise of silence. "There are times when good words are to be left unsaid out of esteem for silence," he writes in chapter 6. "Restraint of Speech." And elsewhere, "Speak no foolish chatter. . . . Do not love quarreling." I think of how many arguments I could have avoided had I stopped myself before spewing out those first angry words "out of esteem for silence."

Every first Sunday of the month, the Mount sisters observe silence from the time they wake until the evening meal. They do not speak in the hallways, their rooms, the dining area, the lounges, or anywhere on the grounds. They call this practice "Sabbath Sunday."

I have looked forward to being at the Mount on a Sabbath Sunday ever since I heard about these silent days. So much of my work involves talking. I ask people questions for a living. I narrate media news reports. I recite my poetry at readings. I give talks to retreat groups. When my workday is over, I crave silence even more than rest.

I've never been one to keep the TV on all day or fill every minute with conversation. Still, I often feel as if I suffer from a silence deficiency. Though I do much of my writing in an attic on a residential street in a small college town, noise is a routine part of my existence. Amtrak trains rumble through town with blaring whistles. My cell phone and house phones ring. Sometimes at the same time. A constant stream of e-mails forms a kind of visual noise. Noise is not just a problem in my little corner of the world. Researchers have found that in 1968, it took fifteen hours of recording time to obtain a single hour of undisturbed nature sounds—birds chirping, wind blowing through trees—without the intrusion of a car starting up, an airplane passing overhead, or some other man-made sound. Today, it takes two thousand hours of recording time to get that one hour of nature sounds.

At first, the silence in the monastery seems strange, especially in the dining room, a place that usually buzzes with several dozen simultaneous conversations and occasional peals of laughter. Today, people sit alone or in pairs at tables that usually seat six. If they linger, they do so to stare out the large bay windows at the patio gardens.

Theirs is not the chilly silence that sometimes wedges between my husband and me when we've had a disagreement. It isn't the lonely silence of walking into a dark hotel room after a long day of work on the road. It isn't the forced silence of taking a test or even the hushed silence of a church sanctuary. This silence is like a communal prayer.

Not talking or listening to someone else talk, I notice things I previously missed. A band of feather reed grass has sprouted up outside the dining room since my last visit. A sparrow's nest sits wedged in a pear tree.

This afternoon, when I walk through the cemetery, I hear the wind exhaling through the pines. I notice how water flows freely now through a drain pipe where just a few days ago a shaft of ice froze on the pipe's lip, like a Fu Manchu beard. Swallows fly overhead, forming a question mark. They make a sound like *pss pss* as they pass. It is as if the day itself is speaking to me in its own language. The words of the Psalms return to me: "Day unto day takes up the story. Night unto night makes known the message."

A few days before this Sabbath Sunday, Sister Micaela Randolph of the Mount's retreat center lent me a video called, appropriately enough, *Noise*. The video recalls the scripture passage in which Elijah looks for God, first in a powerful wind, then in an earthquake, then in a raging fire. Finally, Elijah encounters a "still, small voice." In some texts, the Hebrew word translated as "voice," refers not to an audible sound but to silence. Elijah finds God in the quiet. A statement rolls silently across the screen: *Maybe the healing and guidance we desperately need is not going to come from one more conversation, therapy session or self-help book, but from simply listening to the voice of God.*

Sister Micaela offers me a three-fold standard to apply whenever I am about to speak. Is what I am about to say true? Is it kind? Is it necessary? I probably would conclude most of what I say is the truth (or at least the truth as I see it). Some of it—surely too much—is not kind. And if I am really honest, most of what I say in the course of a day is unnecessary.

Slowly, I am beginning to understand what it means to live a more contemplative life. It is perhaps much simpler than I had ever imagined. It is about speaking with greater attentiveness, exhibiting greater esteem for silence. I wonder if, when I return home, I will be able to carve out one day a month for silence, as the sisters do, or even just a few minutes each day, shutting down the computer of my mind to give it a chance to reboot. Perhaps I can set a few simple goals for myself: more listening, more writing, less speaking.

"There is so much talking that goes on that is utterly useless," Thomas Merton wrote after a visit outside of his cloister. "It is in the sky, the sea, the redwoods that you will find answers." In the silence, everything begins to connect.

The Vinedresser's Touch

The Mount's grapevines are among its oldest residents. They date back to the first sisters who arrived in the mid-1800s. The vineyard is small, less than one hundred yards long, and the yield is slight. But it's enough to produce table grapes, several dozen jars of jelly, and communion wine for the yearly Holy Thursday Mass.

Having lived most of my life in large cities, I know next to nothing about how any plant actually grows. I find a willing teacher in Sister Judith Sutera, monastic scholar, author, and editor of a scholarly journal called *Magistra*, which she fondly refers to as a "cure for insomnia." She is also the monastery's vinedresser. "Everything you need to know about the spiritual life," Sister Judith tells me, "you can learn from the vines."

"The vines," she says, while lifting a branch for me to examine, "will grow and grow and can survive just about anything. But they won't produce anything useful without the careful touch of the vinedresser's hand."

She pulls on a branch that's sprouted about ten feet. "See this one?" she asks. "This thing would just go on and on. So in the spring, I have to whack it back to practically nothing. It's drastic revision, like in writing, where you've got all these ideas and you have to whittle them down to an essential few."

Sister Judith is working on a manuscript that she calls *The Vinedresser's Notebook*. She opens her notebook and reads aloud the following observations and tips, which could apply to life as much as vinedressing:

> When cutting a branch, consider past, present, and future. Understand something of your whole plan.
>
> Keep the roots healthy.
>
> Vines live a long time, but they only have energy enough to sustain, feed and nourish a few shoots well.
>
> Be sure there is enough balance.

I think of how often a plea for moderation crops up in *The Rule of St. Benedict*. He makes no excessive demands, eschews over-eating or incessant working, insists on an adequate amount of rest, and makes room for exceptions ("To each one as he had need").

Sister Judith's notebook continues, "Inevitably, some vines die and you will be disappointed. But others will surprise you with their unexpected fullness." Like each year's communion wine. "Inevitably, someone will complain about the taste of the wine. 'Oh, it's too bitter. Oh, it was better last year.' Well, that's precisely the point. The grapes taste differently year to year depending on the soil, the amount of weeds and pests, the weather," Sister Judith says. "These are grapes that come from our own piece of earth. What could be more appropriate for the wine at Eucharist? Hello!"

The next time we are in the choir chapel, Sister Judith points to an image on one of the Atchison blue windows of a tree stump with new shoots sprouting from its center. Beneath it are the words *Succisa virescit*. "Cut down, it will grow stronger."

"This isn't just about grapes, is it?" I say to Sister Judith.

"No," she responds with a laugh. "Come with me."

We return to the vineyard to trim the wild hops that have become entangled with the branches. Hops look benign enough, like a species of prairie grass, but contain tiny, razor-sharp thorns. With small pairs of shears, Sister Judith and I snip away. We trim the vine's branches too so that the clusters of green grapes beginning to form can receive additional sunlight.

I suggest to her that monastic life is a bit like dressing the vines. It asks us to cut out what's not essential. "Monastic life should be the opposite of the world's tendency to say, 'I want it all, and I want it now,'" Sister Judith says. "The questions we should be asking are, 'Do I need this? Do I need it now? And do I need this much of it?'"

I think of how attached I am to my possessions: certain poetry books, the leather jacket I bought in Italy (a rare extravagance), the diamond earrings I inherited from my grandmother. The Mount sisters go through their closets at least once a year to see what items they can give away or recycle. I do the same periodically, though I am just as likely to pull things out of the box before it gets to Goodwill as I am to put more items in.

After my mother died and we readied my parents' home for sale, I watched as volunteers from Catholic Charities carted off the living room furniture—the couch my mother constantly worried would get a stain, the coffee table we dared not set a glass on for fear it would leave a mark. I know deep down that the possessions that mean so much to me now will one day be thrown out, given away, or carried off to some charity. Still, I hold on tightly.

Succisa virescit. "Cut down, it will grow stronger." The grapevines offer their portion of *conversatio*, if only I'd listen.

Atchison

If we're lucky in life, we may be able to call many places home. There is the place where we grow up: the home we may move from but in our psyche never leave. There are the homes we adopt. For me, that would be Chicago, where I have spent most of my adult life and the major part of my career. And there are places where we land along a journey of discovery that become spiritual homes. I could not have guessed that journey would lead me to a place as unfamiliar as Atchison.

I have been coming to Atchison for several months, but I feel as if I am just getting to know it. Atchison just might be the greatest American city most Americans will never see.

Perhaps I've come to love it so much because, like the two Benedictine monasteries that anchor it, Atchison faltered several times in its history and simply refused to die.

In some ways, the city has lived several lives. Walking along the Missouri River, you can close your eyes and envision wagon trains passing. You can imagine the calls of stevedores and the hiss of steam engines as railroads eventually replaced stagecoaches and steamships. At one time, eight railroad lines terminated here. And all mail headed west passed through Atchison. A sign at the postal depot read, *Needed: Young Men to Ride the Pony Express (Orphans Preferred).*

As writer and native son Thomas Frank points out, Kansas is the place where Superman grows up, Bonnie and Clyde steal a car, Elmer Gantry studies the Bible, and Dorothy struggles to return. It's not hard to imagine any of them settling down at some point in Atchison.

For many (like me before I came here), Atchison registers mainly as one of the trio of cities named in a Johnny Mercer–Harry Warren tune. Today, the Burlington Northern Santa Fe and Union Pacific railroads still grind along the same ballast beds as their famous predecessor. They no longer carry passengers looking westward to a new life; they transport coal and grain mostly. Still, in the wail of their whistles and the roar of their diesel engines as they chug into town, you can step inside Mercer's lyrics as though it was the early 1900s again:

> See the ol' smoke risin' 'round the bend
> I reckon that she knows she's gonna meet a friend
> Folks around these parts get the time of day
> From the Atchison Topeka and the Santa Fe.

The town was named for the well-known slavery advocate David Atchison, a senator from across the border in Missouri. David Atchison had the completely random honor of being president pro tempore of the US Senate when both President-elect Zachary Taylor and his vice president refused to take the oath of office on the Sabbath. As the third-ranking official in government, Atchison claimed to be in charge. And though there isn't a shred of evidence to support it, Atchison's tombstone proclaims him *President of the United States for a Day*. His home in La Platte purports to house "the world's smallest presidential library."

When Mother Evangelista Kremmeter and the first Mount sisters arrived here at the height of the Civil War, they might just as well have landed in Oz. Bloody fighting gripped much of the rest of the nation. But Atchison's residents were busy laying down sidewalks to accommodate their growing population and commercial interests. Of more immediate concern than Confederate marauders was a handful of vociferous Protestants who feared that Catholic education did not compute with an American education. The sisters reassured parents with their textbooks and needlework, promising to teach the young women of Atchison to read, write, paint, stitch, and play musical instruments. A more insidious threat was starvation. In one of her earliest letters, Mother Evangelista exhorted a friend in Minnesota to, "Pray often for me on your knees."

Atchison may have escaped the Civil War relatively unscathed, but the battle over slavery left scars. The aptly named Division Street eventually became a Maginot line separating the races. Atchison's public high school was never segregated, but many taverns and restaurants refused to serve blacks. At one point in the late 1950s, students at St. Benedict's College (now Benedictine College) walked out of a popular tavern and dance hall in protest when the owner refused to serve a black football player. The protest leader was Dick Homan, Sister Thomasita's older brother.

Like the city's sturdy bluffs, black Atchison managed to endure—and thrive. At one time, Emma Covington was the only woman in America, black or white, to own and operate a service station. In a stroke of marketing ingenuity, the city's only African American pharmacist, Leon Henderson, ensured crossover business from whites by opening his store at any hour to fill emergency prescriptions. An African American obstetrician named Dr. George A. Patton gave every baby he delivered a $5 bill as a down payment on the child's education. Elijah Cluke is said to have written the hymn "Just a Closer Walk with Thee" in the men's room of the LFM locomotive finishing plant where he often went to escape his coworkers' taunts.

Atchison began a slow economic slide around 1900. But the town would reinvent itself several times by latching onto new industries as old ones died. One of those industries sprang up by accident of birth. Atchison happens to be the hometown of the legendary aviatrix Amelia Earhart, who liked to tell admirers, "I'm just a girl from Kansas." From her bedroom window, the young Amelia peered out over the bluffs, bursting with the urge to fly. Now every July, thousands of aviation enthusiasts arrive in Atchison for the annual Amelia Earhart Festival.

In the early 1970s, Atchison had the foresight to become one of the first cities in America to design an auto-free zone in its downtown. Unfortunately, few businesses populate Atchison's downtown. The city doesn't yet have a Costco or a Trader Joe's. But it has a Wal-Mart, and until recently, it also had an honest-to-goodness drugstore soda fountain.

While Atchison can boast of some lovely turn-of-the-century homes, whole neighborhoods in the city look as though they need an immediate facelift. Ironically, Atchisonians need look no further than one of their neighbors for home refurbishing tips. Mary Carol Garrity, a third-generation Atchisonian, is the founder of Nell Hill's, one of the foremost home decorating businesses in the country. Busloads of women pour into Atchison weekly to visit Garrity's 130-year-old Greek revival home and buy her books. Garrity says her goal is always "casual sophistication." Same as Atchison's.

The city has a penchant for churning out vivid characters. One of my favorites is William M. "Deafy" Boular. Deafy Boular wasn't only deaf, he was legless too—the result of a train accident when he was ten. A bricklayer, he paved most of Atchison by rolling around on a wooden platform on wheels. When the city tore up some of its streets a few years back, Deafy's bricks sold for $100 apiece as keepsakes. One of them sits on my mantle at home, a gift from Sister Thomasita.

In 1900, Deafy laid forty-six thousand bricks in less than eight hours, a feat no person has ever matched. It earned him a mention in *Ripley's Believe It or Not!* In his compact, challenged body, Deafy seemed to typify the Kansan state motto:

Ad astra per aspera. "To the stars through adversity." A fair description of Atchison and of the Mount sisters, too.

IV.

Seeking Grace

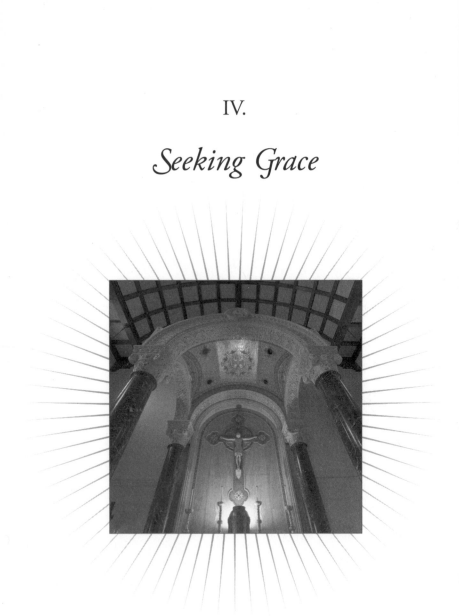

THE CRACKED WATER POT

A water bearer in India had two large pots. Each hung on the end of a pole, which he carried across his neck. One of the pots was perfect and always delivered a full portion of water at the end of a long walk from the stream to the master's house. The other pot had a crack in it and arrived only half full.

For a full two years, this went on daily, with the bearer delivering only one and a half pots of water to the master's house. Of course, the perfect pot was proud of its accomplishments. It succeeded at the purpose for which it was made. But the poor cracked pot was ashamed of its imperfection and considered it a bitter failure that it was able to accomplish only half of what it was created to do. In its embarrassment, the cracked pot spoke one day to the water bearer.

"I am ashamed of myself and want to apologize to you," it said.

"Why?" asked the bearer. "Of what are you ashamed?"

"I have been able for these past two years to deliver only half my load because this crack in my side causes water to leak out."

The water bearer felt sorry for the old cracked pot, and in his compassion, said, "As we return to the master's house, I want you to notice the beautiful flowers along the path."

Indeed, as they went up the hill, the cracked pot noticed the sun warming several bright flowers. The sight of the flowers cheered the pot.

At the end of the trail, the water bearer asked the pot, "Did you notice that there were flowers only on your side of the path and not on the other pot's side? That's because I have always known about your flaw and took advantage of it. I planted seeds on your side of the path, and every day when we walk back from the stream, you water them. For two years, I have been able to pick beautiful flowers to decorate my master's table. If you were not the way you are, he would not have this beauty to grace his house."

—Wisdom Story
as told by Sister Lillian Harrington, "Pilgrim Minister"

Night Shift

The Mount is an unusual religious community in that nearly a quarter of its 145 members are under the age of fifty-five. That might not sound like much, but compared to most monasteries, the Mount is a youth camp. The seventy-year-olds look and act as if they are fifty. The ninety-year-olds could light a city grid with their energy. This is the place to stare down a fear of aging.

The Dooley Center, the Mount's assisted living wing, connects to the rest of the monastery through a hallway. But in many ways, it is a world apart. The retired sisters who live in Dooley have separate meal times and hours for community prayers and Mass. Some are ambulatory but frail, such as Sister Lillian. Others are bedridden. Several are lost in dementia. They too form part of the soul of the monastery.

When I arrive for the night shift, a thin, elderly sister is sitting in a wheelchair near the nurses' station. Sister Phyllis Dye has large eyes a deep shade of blue and the affectless expression of a person lost in an intensely private world. Sister Thomasita walks over to her and inquires cheerfully, "Phyllis, remember when we were out on mission together . . . ?"

Sister Phyllis stares blankly ahead. Sister Thomasita keeps smiling and talking. Sister Phyllis's mind is somewhere perhaps but just not here. As Sister Thomasita waves goodbye to her friend, there are tears in her eyes.

Because it is only 7:00 p.m., too early for bed, several of the Dooley residents congregate around the nurses' station. One of them, Sister Carmel,* eases herself into the chair behind the nurses' desk. She repeatedly folds a large white handkerchief

* This sister's name has been changed to protect her privacy.

into thirds and then sixths. She says (to no one in particular) that she is demonstrating how to fold paper onto which photographs can be pasted. She seems quite unaware she is folding a handkerchief and not a piece of paper. Sister Carmel had served as a school administrator for forty years and had been known as a brilliant educator.

On a previous occasion, I met her walking in the hallway of Dooley with a raincoat draped over her arm.

"Where are you headed in such rain, Sister?" I asked.

"I've got to pick up the students," she said. "They're coming home from a field trip."

Just then an alarm sounded, triggered by the bracelet she wears to alert the staff if she tries to wander outside. A few seconds later, a nurse arrived to escort her away from the door. Tonight she is too absorbed in folding her handkerchief to attempt an escape. Behind Sister Carmel, an episode of *Law and Order: Special Victims Unit* blares from a wide-screen TV, the volume turned way up for the sisters who are hard of hearing. Every few minutes, a commercial for Cialis comes on, promising help for erectile dysfunction.

Soon, another elderly sister inches her way down the hallway with the aid of a walker. She has silver hair swept up in a French twist. Despite her advanced age, she is beautiful, with large brown eyes and the type of classic profile you see on women's faces on Grecian urns. Her name is Sister Helen Buening.

"Have you had a good day, Sister?" one of the nurses asks.

"As always," Sister Helen says. Her voice is barely above a whisper. "What more can I want than to have such wonderful care from people like you?" She lets go of her walker with one arm and reaches over to touch the nurse's cheek. "When I see you, I see Christ," Sister Helen says.

I accompany Sister Helen on her short walk. She tells me she is ninety-two, a retired teacher and artist. Her "fire and clay" retreats once drew hundreds of artists to the monastery. She says this is the first time in weeks she's felt up to walking. She has just finished reading a book about a Rwandan woman who spent months in hiding with other women in a cramped bathroom, praying for an end to the genocide that had already taken several of her family members. Sister Helen can't remember the title, but she tells me, "You must read this woman's book. Her whole life was built on faith."

Her whole life was built on faith. That could be said of any of the Mount sisters. When Sister Helen tires, I escort her back to her room. It occurs to me that I've seen her once before. One day, as I was passing the Dooley Center chapel, the nurses wheeled her into Mass on a hospital bed. She was wearing an eye mask, I supposed, because too much light hurts her eyes. I remember looking at her and thinking, *What a miserable existence.*

Sister Helen's room is down the hall from Sister Kathleen Egan's. I ask the nurses if they think it's too late for me to have a quick visit with Sister Kathleen. They tell me it shouldn't be a problem. Sister Kathleen stays up late watching cable news.

When I knock on her door, she's sitting upright in an easy chair, dressed in a crisp blue business suit. Her face looks thinner than I remember from the last time I saw her, but her skin has that same translucence, her eyes the same light. She tells me one of the sisters from Dooley died a few weeks ago and that another is quite ill in the hospital.

"The next step for us is heaven," she says softly. "I don't mind, really. I'm ready. The sooner the better as far as I'm concerned. When you live over here, you get to where you look around the room and wonder, 'Who will be next?' We have these little place cards on the dining room tables, and as people die, the other place cards get moved around. It's quite a thing."

A nurse's aide arrives to take Sister Kathleen's vital signs, and I bid her goodnight. I think about those shifting name tags on the dinner table. How real and yet how utterly inconceivable it is to think about the day I too will no longer exist, not even as a name on a place card at a table.

When I return to the nurses' station, Sister Sylvia Kenkel is about to dole out the evening medications. "Sylvia has walked more people to eternity than anyone I know," Sister Thomasita had told me. When we arrive at Sister Phyllis's bedroom, she is lying on her side, her eyes wide open, staring at the wall. A poster of the Foggy River Boys and a photograph of John Paul II riding in his "Popemobile" hang on her closet door.

"Open up for medicine," Sister Sylvia says cheerily. But Sister Phyllis tightens her lips.

"C'mon now, Phyllis, offer it to Jesus," Sister Sylvia says by way of encouragement. But the woman in the bed does not budge. You have to wonder what dream of reality is going on behind those large blue eyes.

"I'll mark down 'refused medicine,'" Sister Sylvia says. "We don't force things on anybody." The sisters sign do-not-resuscitate orders, she explains, and decline any extraordinary measures to keep them alive. I find that stunning. I think people should fight to their last drop of energy to hold on to life. *Rage, rage against the dying of the light.*

"This is the part of the monastery that is shielded from the world," Sister Sylvia had said to me when the shift began. And yet, something about these women—weak, befuddled, and ready as they are to die—seems to me like prayer.

By 11:00 p.m., the center is quiet. The medicine has been doled, vital signs recorded, the TV set muted. The sisters disappear into their rooms and settle down to sleep. As I walk back to the main monastery, a nurse runs up to me with a slip of paper. Sister Helen has remembered the title of the book by the Rwandan civil war survivor and written it down: *Left to Tell.* I have to smile. If there's any reason for having writers in the world, it is likely this: Someone has to live to tell these stories. Perhaps that is the gift I can offer these sisters.

A Notebook

I sometimes imagine that the moment of death is like the final scene in the film *Looking for Mr. Goodbar.* Diane Keaton's character, Theresa, is beaten to death by a drifter. The room she dies in turns to black. The movie screen goes blank. We move with the character from life to nothingness.

For some reason, that scene comes to mind when I return to my room after spending the night shift at the Dooley Center. I find it hard to sleep. The next day, Sister Thomasita asks me what I thought of the experience. I tell her it made me sad—and angry. Angry that women who had dedicated their lives to serving others now had to suffer the indignity of dementia and painful physical conditions. And sad that so many of them seemed resigned to merely waiting to die, their do-not-resuscitate orders on file.

"I have something to show you," Sister Thomasita said after a long pause. "They're notes I took when I was sitting with my good friend Sister Mary Noel during the last two months of her life." Sister Mary Noel had died in 1978 of bone cancer at the age of fifty-two. "I kept this notebook during the time she and I experienced her death and life. I think they offer the real thing."

Sister Thomasita may also have had in mind my father's recent death in wanting me to see the notebook. I don't know what I expected, but it was not the gripping narrative I was about to read:

> I know of no beauty compared with the painful beauty of this past week with Sister M. Noel. She shared with us an experience she had had as a young college student, when what she called "the flaming magnificence of autumn" caught her and held her. "I looked," she said, "at one particularly beautiful leaf as it slowly drifted to the ground. I picked it up and questioned how it had become so uniquely glorious. I realized that the leaf became beauty in its ready acceptance of all of life—wind, rain, sunshine. It ripened, taking in fully what was its life. And then when it had to, it had let go. It had opened itself completely to the Creator. I knew then that in my life I must do the same. The time would come too, to let go. . . . "

The entries in the notebook continue:

This week Sister M. Noel began singing this verse from Psalm 121: "I rejoiced when I heard them say, let us go to the house of the Lord. And now our feet are standing within your gates, O Jerusalem. . . . "

She asked me to join her in singing and praying. She remarked that her feet were right at the gates of Jerusalem, but not yet *within*. Two days ago, late at night, her face suddenly smoothed into a joyful expression as her eyes focused on the right side of her bed. I was the only other person in the room. She turned to me and asked, "What time did they say the reunion will be?"

I asked, "Who? What reunion?"

"The reunion the two sisters just invited me to—Sisters Malachy and Madonna."

Malachy and Madonna had been her good friends and colleagues at Benedictine College. They had died years before.

A few more days pass, then this entry:

Sister Mary Noel prayed much this week, but since she sleeps more and more, her concept of time is interesting. Frequently on awakening, she suggests we pray Morning Praise. We pray it at various hours: 5:00 p.m., 1:00 a.m., 3:00 a.m., 11:00 p.m. It's been some time since we've prayed Evening Praise. Her days are filled with mornings, beginnings.

Sister Mary Noel's condition steadily worsens, according to Sister Thomasita's notebook:

Throwing her arms around my neck and pulling my head down toward her, she whispered in my ear: "Talk to me about death and separation." We talked of God being Love itself, therefore any love we now have must be of its very essence ever-present. Complete and eternal union with God would also mean presence to ALL loved ones. We talked about how the leap to greater presence involved passing through pain, but that it indeed was a "passing through."

We talked of an absence of the long days and nights of leg pains, nausea, dryness, periodic disorientation, weakness, and waiting. We talked of the hundred-fold increase of the type of vigor and vitality she used to experience in her tennis games. We wept much. We prayed for eyes that could see and hearts that could reach. When we would stop momentarily, she'd whisper: "That's beautiful. Don't stop. Say more. Please keep talking." And we did.

Sister Mary Noel died shortly after that entry was written. It was December 8, the Feast of the Immaculate Conception. A few days before, she told Sister Thomasita that she dreamt she had attended a homecoming game at the college where she'd been president. She tried to take an empty seat in the bleachers, but it was too small for her. She started to leave the stadium, disappointed that she would have to miss the game. Then she noticed a crowd waiting for her on the field and a sign that said HOMECOMING in huge, bright lettering. Again she saw an empty seat. She walked over to it and sat down. "It's going to be a good fit," Sister Mary Noel said later, recalling the dream. "A *homecoming* fit."

I don't doubt that in letting me read her notebook, Sister Thomasita wanted me to see that there are other views of death besides my own morose version of a movie screen going dark. In Sister Mary Noel's case, her dying appeared to be a journey, one where her dreams, her conversations, even her waking visions of those who had preceded her in death served as markers on the path to her new destination. After my father died, I lay on his bed trying to imagine what he had seen in those last moments of consciousness: the odd crack in the ceiling, the line of family photographs on his bureau, or perhaps a vision seen only by him. *His* homecoming.

In the early 1990s, I wrote a front page story for the *Wall Street Journal* about Duncan Henderson, a retired, religiously conservative business executive who had cared for his son, who was dying of AIDS. Paul Henderson was bedridden for several weeks before his death, but he told his friends of soaring above his neighborhood on the northwest side of Chicago. He said he could see his parents going about their daily chores. He described events that, while confined to his bed, he could not possibly have seen. "The line between life and death," Paul said, "is thinner than you think."

Perhaps eternity is not some destination we barrel toward, but part of the here and now and the future too, all of it connected by a single thread—what the author John O'Donohue called "unbroken presence." The life and passion of a person "leave an imprint on the ether of a place," O'Donohue writes in *Anam Cara*, like "secret tabernacles in a landscape." The narrative of Sister Mary Noel's last days suggests as much too.

I don't know whether that's wishful fantasy or not. I'd like to believe it's true. It's certainly more comforting than contemplating that blank movie screen. For now, I can only "take in fully" all that is my life. At its end, I hope that I will be like the leaf Sister Mary Noel saw in autumn, fully ripened and ready to let go. I think of a line from the poet Rumi:

"Everyone's death is of the same quality as himself: to the enemy of God, an enemy; to the friend of God, a friend."

Peppermint Schnapps and Ashes

At the Mount, work often spills into prayer, prayer flows into rest, and silence into laughter. There is time to contemplate weighty matters and time to just have fun in equal measure. On the evening I finish reading the notebook about Sister Mary Noel, the monastery celebrates Mardi Gras. The dining room tables sparkle with centerpieces of green, purple, and gold beads, which the sisters amuse themselves trying on. After dinner, we walk over to the community room at the nursing care center where large trays of beignets sit alongside coffee vats full of hot cocoa. But this is no ordinary cocoa. It's spiked with peppermint schnapps.

I sit at a table next to Sister Celinda Medina, who has been confined to a wheelchair ever since her surgeon's hand slipped and damaged a nerve in her back. The monastery could have filed a malpractice suit, but Sister Celinda refused to take legal action. Her young surgeon had offered a tearful apology. She didn't want to jeopardize his future career. I once suggested to Sister Mary Agnes, who had been the prioress at the time, that the sisters might have tried to negotiate a financial settlement with the doctor for damages even if they didn't want to sue him. "For what?" she asked with a shrug. "To get a bunch of money?"

Sister Celinda breaks off a bit of beignet and with a gnarled and shaking hand, dips it into her hot cocoa. She spends her days now piecing together intricate puzzles. She tells me to be sure to check out her latest, a one thousand-piece image of the Virgin Mary. When I ask how she manages to finish such intricate pieces, she merely smiles. The sister sitting next to her leans toward me conspiratorially and whispers, "She gets a lot of help from the nurses."

Everyone is talking and having a grand time, filling one another's cups with cocoa and peppermint schnapps. I think of the care *The Rule* takes in assigning certain hours for rest, for reading, for relaxation, and of how the Benedictines view leisure too as holy. Then, at the appointed time, the laughter winds down. The room becomes silent. In front of the fireplace lay fronds from last year's Palm Sunday Mass.

Sister Alberta Hermann lights the hearth, and one by one the sisters cast these palm branches into the flames. They will become the ashes for tomorrow's service. We say a prayer, promising to give "strength and support to one another on the Lenten journey to the Easter Triduum." We sing, "All creatures of our God and King lift up your voice and hear us sing. Alleluia, Alleluia." It is the last time the alleluia will be uttered until Holy Saturday. For the rest of the evening until the end of Ash Wednesday the next day, there is silence in the monastery. Laughter to silence. Leisure to prayer. Life to death. Death to life.

Remember, you are dust, and unto dust you shall return. The sisters use the more traditional and sober prayer for applying ashes. An alternate prayer reads a bit less morbidly: *Turn away from sin and listen to the Good News of the Gospel.* The one I like best, though, is the version my husband's small faith group used one year, adapted from a line of Robert Frost's: *Turn away from sin and take the road less traveled.* That the monastery would use something more sober makes sense. There's no sugarcoating here: The Mount sisters see reality in all its intensity.

I receive my ashes—as a cross upon the forehead—from Sister Mary Elizabeth Schweiger, the Mount's subprioress. Sister Mary Liz was one of the first sisters I encountered on my initial visit to the Mount. When I walked into the guest quarters, I noticed several women in the common area playing cards and enjoying a few glasses of wine. One of them rose immediately to greet me.

"Are you here on a weekend retreat?" I asked her.

"Oh no, I'm the subprioress of the monastery," she said. I laughed at my ready assumption that someone enjoying laughs with friends over a few glasses of wine wouldn't be a member of the monastic community.

If a monastery's prioress is similar to a chief executive officer, the subprioress is more like the chief operating officer, responsible for day-to-day operations. She is also the sounding board for suggestions and complaints.

When I ask Sister Mary Liz if her job ever proves stressful, she points to a cabinet in her office that contains a collection of clown dolls. They're her diversion to break the tension whenever a conversation gets overheated. Like her collection of dolls, she aims to be "a non-anxious presence" within the community.

A non-anxious presence. I thought of the former executive editor at the *Washington Post*, who used to say the *Post* ran on "creative tension." He thought that was a good thing. I remembered how stressed I could become as a reporter, all the public relations officers I pestered for information, all the times I had gotten testy with my husband if I thought he wasn't working hard enough on our presentations.

To remain a "non-anxious presence," Sister Mary Liz sets aside one day for herself each week. She doesn't go near the office, but spends time alone carving "comfort crosses," small handheld crosses similar to worry beads. "You have to set boundaries," she says. I thought again of the *Washington Post* and the "model reporter" my editors admired, who worked late into the night and on weekends, eating at his desk, chain-smoking. I wonder if he still works there; I wonder if he is still alive.

When I stand in front of Sister Mary Liz to receive my ashes, I look into her eyes for several seconds. I feel as if I am looking into the eyes of wisdom. She lifts her thumb to lightly trace a cross on my forehead. *Remember, you are dust, and unto dust you shall return.*

Reconciliation

Because ritual is such a rich part of life at the Mount, I find myself drawn anew to Catholic traditions. After spending the first part of Lent at the monastery, I decide to revisit a sacrament I hadn't thought about in years.

Reconciliation, formerly known as "going to Confession," is the Rodney Dangerfield of sacraments. Compared to others, such as Baptism, Marriage, and the Anointing of the Sick, the sacrament of Reconciliation receives scant respect and even less attention from the flock. Untold generations were marred at a tender age by having to step behind a curtain into a dark box, drop to their knees, and admit their most embarrassing flaws to a person seen only in profile from behind a screen. That person, the priest, could pronounce you absolved from your sins or decide you were still a dirty, rotten sinner. He punched your ticket to heaven or hell. The whole experience was even more excruciating if the priest recognized your voice and knew your family, your teachers, or your employer.

It's no wonder many Catholics tossed aside the practice. In the same way that an airline that's had a plane crash will sometimes change its name, the Church rebranded Confession in the 1970s, giving it the more user-friendly name of Reconciliation. Since then, parishes have tried to coax people back by offering something called a "Penance Service," usually during Lent. These services offer a chance to examine the conscience privately. Those who are brave enough can still see a priest individually for Confession (excuse me, Reconciliation).

Two weeks before Easter, I decide to attend the Penance Service at the Franciscan parish I attend when I'm at our home in central Illinois. It's a sparse crowd, about one hundred people in a parish of over a thousand. Sinning apparently isn't as popular a pastime in Bloomington, Illinois, as I had thought.

Printed copies of a suggested examination of conscience are available in the pews. I run down the offered litany of sins. No, I haven't stolen or been dishonest in my dealings with others. No, I haven't cheated on my husband. Yes, I've been insensitive. Yes, I've "torn down rather than built up," as my worship aid puts it.

I had planned to stay for the opening prayer and privately perform the examination of conscience—but not actually confess to a priest. That might be carrying my good intentions too far. But at the sight of all these people lined up to unburden their sins, I too rise from my pew. I join the line waiting for the single confessional box where I won't be seen by my confessor.

This ends up being the longest line and the slowest moving. After about a half hour of waiting, I notice that the people who chose face-to-face confessions finish within a few minutes. They walk breezily out of the church. That convinces me to switch lines.

I hope to confess to someone who doesn't know me, but all the priests here know me by name. I join the line for Father Gregg, a quiet man who spent many years working as a missionary. As a former missionary, I figure he might be more worldly than your average parish priest.

When it's my turn, I slide into a pew beside him. He surprises me by taking my hands in his. He looks at me directly. He asks what I most want to change about myself. I tell him about my bursts of anger and my feelings of resentment against people who've hurt me. We talk about how I wish I had a better relationship with my stepdaughters. I expect him to say something like, "You need to stop that. Try harder." Instead, he looks me in the eye and says, "You're in a difficult situation. Just keep doing the best you can. Keep praying about it."

He asks me to recite the Act of Contrition. It's been so long since I went to Confession that I can't remember all the words to the prayer, so Father Gregg helps me along. "Oh my God, I am heartily sorry for having offended you, and I detest all my sins because I dread the loss of heaven and the pains of hell; but most of all, because they offend you, my God, who are all good and deserving of all my love. . . . " It's humbling to say those words out loud and to acknowledge that things I've done—and haven't done—also end up hurting God who is "all good and deserving of all my love." I feel as if I should add that I'm also "heartily sorry" for having offended *anyone* in my life who is "deserving of all my love."

Father Gregg offers a prayer of absolution. Like the others before me, I walk easily out of the church.

"That Boy"

When I married and began living most of the time in central Illinois, I found parishes in my new diocese generally more conservative than the ones I knew in Chicago. After I had sampled all the parishes in town, I settled on one led by Franciscan priests. The parish has an active group of "Secular Franciscans," lay men and laywomen who seek to follow St. Francis's spirit of service and simplicity. It supports an outreach ministry for people living on the margins in Appalachia. Still, I recognized a streak of conservatism there too. Many people in the parish knew my husband had been married previously. When some friends encouraged me to inquire about joining the lay Franciscan group, one of the first questions I was asked was whether my marriage was "valid" in the Catholic Church.

The answer was yes. Still, I wondered, *What if it wasn't? Does the status of my marriage define the authenticity of my faith?*

Whenever I return home from the Mount, I try to continue the practice I have there of attending daily Mass. One morning during Lent, I went to Mass at my local parish. The celebrant was a generally amiable priest, who nonetheless occasionally had scolded divorced Catholics from the pulpit and complained that not enough parishioners sent their kids to Catholic school. The day's gospel reading told of a blind man whom Jesus restores to sight. Instead of rejoicing, the Pharisees condemn Jesus for healing on the Sabbath. In his homily, the celebrant noted that people in leadership positions were often the most hostile to Jesus' message. *Okay*, I thought, *no argument there.* Then he added, "And if Jesus were to appear in Washington, DC, today—quite frankly—I don't think he would be welcome there either."

After Mass, I followed him into the sacristy to ask what he meant by his remarks. He had just removed his vestments and was placing the altar vessels in a drawer. I tried to sound amused rather than confrontational. He slammed the drawer shut, turned around, and glared at me. "That *boy* is leading this country to hell!" he shouted. Then he stormed out of the sacristy.

It took a few seconds for it to register that this priest had just referred to the first African American president as "that boy." At home that evening, I asked my husband if perhaps there was a kinder interpretation to put on this choice of words. He didn't think so. I thought, *How can I ever take Communion again from that priest?* I thought too about the Mount and how meaningful it is to stand at Mass with women who pray for presidents Republican and presidents Democrat, who don't check credentials at the door. Increasingly, it feels as if the Mount is all I have left of my faith.

Such a Story

It is a relief to once again attend Mass at the Mount. I return on Holy Thursday, where Mass is in the grand St. Scholastica Chapel with its marble columns and soaring stained glass windows depicting women saints. The sisters place several basins of warm water around the altar alongside baskets of towels for the ceremonial foot washing.

In all the years I've attended Mass on Holy Thursday, I've never felt comfortable about this particularly intimate ritual. It's a bit too much like showmanship. Besides, I prefer doing, being the giver, rather than sitting back and letting myself be served. I don't even like watching other people get their feet washed. But I've come to the Mount for *conversatio*, to alter my usual way of thinking.

When there is only one person left in line, I rise from my pew. Like the others ahead of me, I walk barefoot, feeling the cool marble of the chapel under my feet. Walking without shoes feels unnatural, but I suppose that's the point. A woman I don't know, someone at the monastery for a Triduum retreat, washes my feet. "Washing" seems to be too strong a description, "dribbling" would be more like it. The water smells of lavender.

Because there is no one behind me in line, I assume I won't have to wash someone else's feet. *Thank God*, I thought. Then

Sister Mary Liz plops down in the chair in front of me. Pretty soon I am splashing water on the soles of the subprioress's feet. They are noticeably small and delicate. I keep my eyes on my work because, to be quite frank, it is a little disquieting to wash someone else's feet. When I finally look up, she mouths the words, "Thank you."

I've always heard in the readings of Holy Thursday a call to serve, to be a person "of the towel." For the first time, it occurs to me that I also need the humility to let myself be served. We—I—must learn the art of receiving.

As Mass ends, retired Abbot Owen Purcell, who's come from the abbey down the road to preside at the service, and Sister Anne, the prioress, don shoulder vestments and carry the Eucharist through the monastery's corridors. We sing in Latin, *Praestet fides supplementum senseum defectui.* "Faith can see by revelation more than senses ever saw." To see more than the senses can reveal. Isn't that what I've come to this monastery to learn?

Younger sisters bring the wheelchair-bound into the chapel. Another case of giving and receiving. We sit or kneel before the Blessed Sacrament exposed in the tabernacle. Only an occasional cough breaks the silence. Soon, lightning streaks across the chapel's dark windows. Thunder bellows and rain batters the roof. This looks more like Good Friday weather. But here inside this small chapel is serenity, safety, and prayer. How peaceful it is to sit in the dark, listening to the song of thunder and rain.

On most days, a bell calls the community to prayer. But on Good Friday, we rise to pray at a sound like a slap across the face, the *thwack* of a wooden clapper. Like a harbinger, a bare wooden cross sits near the altar.

Sister Diana Seago chants passages from the book of Lamentations: "Against me alone God turns again and again the whole day long. . . . Jerusalem, Jerusalem. . . ." By contrast, the spring day seems to be singing alleluias. The storms of the night have passed, and the sun is a dollop of butter in the southern sky. The dogwood trees shimmer in pink. None of them evoke the wood of the cross. Starlings call to one another in high-pitched voices. Unlike the sisters, the birds do not observe Good Friday silence.

At 3 o'clock, we gather to venerate the cross. The crucifixion narrative is so familiar, it's tempting to tune out whole sections of it. Still, each year, some new detail pops out at me. This time, I zero in on the story's many bit players and secondary characters and try to imagine the backstories of their lives. The unnamed bystander who loses his loincloth running from the authorities. Malchus, the high priest's servant whose ear Peter cuts. Dismas, the released prisoner whose final words to Christ, "Jesus, remember me when you come into your kingdom," we still say today. Simon the Cyrenian, who helps carry the Cross. And Joseph of Arimathea, who just happens to have a burial plot available when Jesus needs one.

There is also the specificity of incidental details. Judas turns Jesus over to the authorities not with a handshake or a nod or an embrace but with a *kiss*. At one point, Pilate asks, "What is truth?" You have to wonder why anyone would include these odd details if they weren't the truth.

"Who would believe what we have just heard?" Sister Anne asks in her reflection on the Passion narrative. "After a meal with friends, an innocent man is marched off to his death, unjustly accused, pushed into the hands of politicians who have no backbone, scourged by soldiers doing what they were told to do, and cared for after death by a man too timid to speak to him in the daylight."

Yes, who would believe such a story? "Victims of trafficking, of unjust prison sentencing, or illegal search and seizures—they would believe what we heard in the reading. And billions more throughout the world who suffer needless arrest, torture, and death," she says.

As we stand for the petitions, we pray for the Jewish people, *the first to hear the word of God*; for all Muslims, *that they may find joy and peace in their firm belief in our one God who has many names*; for those with special needs, *that God will bring healing and peace to all who suffer from war, violence, and natural disasters*; and finally, for the planet on which we live, *that the fragility, interdependence, majesty, and wonder of creation may be cherished by all.*

To the relentless beat of a kettle drum, several sisters lift a large wooden cross and carry it to the center of the altar. Another walks ahead, stopping every few feet to circle the air with a clay pot filled with incense. Ever since I was a child and attended my first Good Friday service, veneration of the cross has brought me to the brink of tears. Perhaps it is the act of stooping down and kissing a cross in public, an act that seems so private, that I find deeply humbling. We line up two by two and advance toward the altar. I feel as if I am walking with women who, two thousand years ago, could have been the ones weeping as a battered, bloody Jesus stumbled past them.

I notice that many of the sisters wrap their hands around the cross as they bend down to kiss it. I think, *This is what it means to defeat suffering: embrace it, bow to it, kiss it, overcome it with love.* We sing the powerful words of the hymn "What Wondrous Love Is This?" *And when from death I'm free, I'll sing on, I'll sing on. And through eternity, I'll sing on.*

I look to see who is walking beside me. It is Sister Lillian, one of my first friends at the Mount, a woman who has spent more than seventy years walking toward the cross. I am honored to put my lips to the cross she has kissed before me.

Later, when the rest of the monastery returns to silence, I see Sister Lillian from a distance, reading to her sister Mary. I can make out only a few of the words she is saying. But at that moment, in the quiet of the monastery, her clear, comforting voice seems to me the most beautiful sound in the world.

Hookups and Holy Week

Returning to my home life after an extended period at the Mount always requires some adjustment. My re-entry after Holy Week feels particularly abrupt. I would like to luxuriate in the memory of the Triduum liturgies, Easter's comforting promise that the result of acute suffering is life, and the end of life is actually *more life*. But work howls for my attention, specifically an assignment for PBS-TV on the "hookup" culture.

For the uninitiated (and believe me, you're lucky if you are), hookups are what have largely replaced traditional dating on college campuses. Hookups skip the intermediary steps of courtship and go straight to the endgame. There's sexual intimacy but with no relationship, no emotional connection, and certainly no commitment.

Throughout Holy Week, I'd read student accounts of their hookup adventures. One young man told of wearing "beer goggles," being so drunk he couldn't see the person he was having sex with. Another described a "Date Auction" in which women parade across a catwalk in their bra and underwear while male students bid on spending the night with them. I wonder whether I'm adding anything to "the soul of the world," as writer Paulo Coehlo puts it, by broadcasting such stupid behavior on national TV.

The day after Easter also happens to be my husband's birthday. I would like to spend it with him. Instead, I drive to South Bend, Indiana, to interview a sociologist at the University of Notre Dame who's been following the lives of young adults over the course of several years. Then I fly to Dallas for some additional interviews, which means eating alone that night in some unfamiliar restaurant and returning to an empty hotel room.

Even more depressing are the interviews with the students. A rather earnest young man at Southern Methodist University says of hookups, "I think it's better than having a relationship. There's more excitement. You don't have the monotony of going to dinner with the same girl." He adds, "Every girl is like a flower. You never see an ugly flower. So you see all these girls, these flavors, and you want to taste all of them." With that comment, even our usually stone-faced producer bursts out laughing. I merely feel sad, both for this young man and for the women who have to seek their life partners from the current gene pool.

The next day, as I sit in Dallas–Fort Worth Airport, breathing in the stale air and watching perspiring people rush by with their rolling bags, I begin thinking about the choices that the Mount sisters have made. I arrive at the monastery with all the conventional ideas about monastic life. I think it a worthwhile occupation for a few hardy souls, but a hopelessly outmoded one. A laywoman can have a deep prayer life if she chooses. She can perform the same church ministries as a monastic woman. And she doesn't have to take a vow of obedience, forgo marriage and family life, or renounce personal wealth to do it.

But who has chosen the better life? I think it again when I am back in Chicago, returning home from the airport on a subway train so crowded I can tell what the person next to me ate for lunch. And again, as I juggle my rolling suitcase and shoulder bag in a public elevator reeking of urine and vomit. One can do worse than choose monastic life: to live in the midst of nature, to note the hours, to die surrounded by community, to pursue what really matters.

Who has chosen the better part?

Dancing a Jitterbug

I have been feeling an increasing sense of alienation from my work as a journalist, as if I'm merely sleepwalking through my assignments. Instead of nourishing a sense of the sacred, work often interferes with prayer and leaves me too depleted to notice the sacred in anything. I ask Sister Thomasita if she thinks a person can live a contemplative life outside of a monastic setting. That's when she tells me about dancing a jitterbug.

"Some of my most contemplative moments have come to me when I'm dancing," she says, throwing her head back and laughing. "I used to dance the jitterbug all the time in high school. In the movement of the dance, I would experience this sudden moment of interior pause. I could feel the presence of God."

I think of the scene in the film *Chariots of Fire* where a deeply devout young runner tells his teammate, "When I run, I breathe in God." Perhaps you don't have to carve out special "contemplative time." Perhaps you don't even have to be still.

"Sometimes in our day-to-day life and activities, we can experience God even more intensely than here in the monastery," Sister Thomasita adds. "It's often the times when we feel completely empty or when we think we've turned completely from God that we'll find God. I tell people to look for the coldest and the hottest moments in your life. Look carefully at those moments. God is there."

My work as a journalist accounts for some of the coldest moments lately—my assignment on the hookup culture being a prime example. But looking back, I see there were other assignments I wouldn't have traded—stories that put me in touch with extraordinary people doing important work. Kris and Ray Hallowell, funeral directors who have led a grief recovery group at no charge for the past twenty years.

Jerry Hiller and his wife, Marilyn Rochon, counselors who offer free lunchtime sessions in a church basement for workers coping with job loss or the conflicting demands of work and family. Gwen and David Clayborne, who grew up in the segregated South and now, in their retirement, bring people of diverse races, religions, and backgrounds together once a month for a meal at their home.

Telling their stories reminds me of why I became a journalist. Those experiences left me neither hot nor cold, but inspired. Sister Thomasita was right. God was there in every one of those people and, by extension, in my work. I can return to the monastery when I feel the need for a tune-up, but I can also look to the people I meet in the day-to-day course of my work. They too can lead me to the sacred.

Consensus

Monasteries are among the world's oldest continuous enterprises. They've endured for more than 1,500 years, so there's got to be some practical wisdom there. In the eighteenth century, Emperor Joseph II decided monasteries were useless, inefficient ventures and tried to close 867 of them in Europe. But monastic life ended up outlasting both the emperor and his empire.

As enterprises, monasteries share a number of similarities with small corporations. Both must respond to changing cycles. At the Mount, the sisters built in times of expansion, and when buildings were no longer needed, they closed them, sold them, or tore them down, recycling what they could and burying the rest in their own land. The community enjoyed surplus budgets some years and stared down financial ruin in others. When necessary, the Mount spun off daughter houses or merged with other monasteries to survive. And yet, monasteries also behave in ways largely counter to conventional business practices.

For months now, I've been hearing terms like "consultation," "collegiality," and "consensus" to describe how significant decisions are made. The goal is to arrive at a course of action the entire community can support. How different that seems from the top-down corporate model of decision making I have experienced in the business world.

November 15, 1993, is a date etched in my memory. On that morning, I strolled as usual into the London bureau of the *Wall Street Journal*. It was a typical English morning, a mix of sun and clouds, mild for late fall. I glanced out a window at the gray dome of St. Paul's Cathedral, always a comforting sight, and settled in to review the day's news wires. My bureau chief walked over and summoned me into his office. I knew the topic would be serious when he closed the door behind him.

"I have very bad news for you," he began. "the *Journal* is having a layoff, and you're being laid off." My first instinct was to say, "This has got to be a joke." The piece that I had written about a father caring for his son dying of AIDS had recently been a finalist for the Pulitzer Prize in the feature writing category. The article had generated nearly two hundred letters from readers, many of whom said the story had changed forever their perspective on AIDS sufferers.

I could see my bureau chief had typed out on a piece of paper what he planned to say. He began rattling off, "Your termination date is . . . Your severance package is . . ." I remember thinking that it had taken me fifteen years to that point to build my career and fifteen seconds for someone to wipe it all away.

Losing a job is like losing someone close to you. It is also a bit like being the spouse who wants the marriage to continue but is served divorce papers anyway. The term "layoff" is oddly euphemistic, like referring to murder as "population control." The British have a much more apt expression. They call it "being made redundant." It tracks more closely the feelings of worthlessness that spring up when your employer says you are no longer necessary. In a word, redundant.

In the television show *Mad Men*, a hard-drinking advertising executive is told to take time off to dry out. "If I don't show up at the office every day, then who am I?" he asks. I felt much the same way that November morning with so much of my identity invested in being a *Wall Street Journal* reporter. I left the office thinking, *My life is over.* That hardly turned out to be the case, though I couldn't know it then.

The editors took pains to say the layoff was strictly an economic decision, entirely unrelated to my work or that of the other reporters who were let go at the same time. Certain board members and powerful shareholders felt the newspaper's stock was underperforming. They advocated cutting costs to increase profits and drive up the stock price. A quick way to do that was to eliminate jobs.

Chapter 72 of *The Rule of St. Benedict,* "The Good Zeal of Monks," proposes a different way of doing business. "Try to be the first to show respect to the other," St. Benedict says. "No one is to pursue what he judges better for himself, but instead what he judges best for someone else." Could the monastic practice of consensus provide a more just way of arriving at decisions?

The Rule gives the abbot or prioress final say, but it also says *all* should be "called for counsel," regardless of age, position, or seniority. "The reason why we have said all should be called for counsel is that the Lord often reveals what is better to the younger."

When the *Journal* engineered its layoff, employees were never consulted about whether there might be other ways to cut costs. One of the more senior reporters offered to take early retirement to save younger reporters' jobs and suggested others in his age bracket might be willing to do the same. But that was after the fact. Management rebuffed his and other ideas.

Sister Noreen Hurter is a soft-spoken woman with a gentle manner and a ready smile who wears a modified religious habit: a two-piece suit and partial veil. She served as the Mount's prioress in the financially challenging period from 1976 to 1988. By then, the community had dropped from a peak of 600 sisters to 499. Fewer sisters meant fewer people to bring in incomes (from teaching, nursing, etc.) to support the work of the monastery. Sister Noreen often turned to prayer in hopes of balancing the books.

The monastery also faced several emotionally charged choices. One was what to do with the building that once housed Mount St. Scholastica College's administrative offices. In 1971, the sisters had merged their school with St. Benedict's College to form a single co-ed institution, Benedictine College. For many alumnae, the handsome tan brick administration building symbolized the alma mater they had loved and lost in the merger.

Atchison officials also weighed in, seeking to preserve the building as a community center. The problem was, it cost the sisters more to maintain the building than they received in income from the community-based programs it housed.

With a major decision pending, each member of the monastery receives a wide range of information. The books are opened, so to speak. (Would that the *Wall Street Journal* had offered the same courtesy.) Ideas are hashed out in committees, and then a series of open meetings follow in which the entire community discusses the matter. Everyone is "to express their opinions with all humility," *The Rule* says, "and not presume to defend their own views obstinately." By contrast, when I covered business stories for the *Journal*, I often witnessed how a small group of people—a few top managers, a handful of board members, or some disgruntled shareholders—could drive decisions that affected thousands of workers and, by extension, thousands of customers.

Interestingly, Sister Noreen found herself on the opposing side in the decision to raze the college's administration building. An outside consultant had recommended bulldozing not only the administration building but two others structures as well, including St. Scholastica Chapel, considered by many to be the Mount's architectural jewel. It became increasingly clear something had to go. Ultimately, Sister Noreen lent her support, too, to what the rest of the community thought best. "You see where the will of the people is going. And even though you think you're right, there's no reason to keep standing up and saying no." But it wasn't simply a case of majority rules. The process continued until the dissenters also felt comfortable with the decision. In a word, *consensus*.

"In community life, we don't take a vote and one side wins and the other side loses," explains Sister Mary Agnes, another former prioress. "We try to approach issues as a sharing of our wisdom. You put your wisdom out there, and then you let go of it. You try to listen to everybody. Then you take time and pray.

"If two-thirds of the community is leaning one way and I'm leaning another, I've got to ask myself, 'Where does God seem to be leading me?' If everybody else is going in a different direction than I am, then I need to say, 'Is there some wisdom in their way?'"

"Isn't there a danger that a 'herd mentality' will set in and stifle dissenters who raise legitimate issues?" I ask.

"We address the concerns of those in dissent. We do that a lot," Sister Mary Agnes says. "I don't think we ever say that because the majority is going one way, forget about the others. Even if the group is going a particular way, we'll say, 'Well, what about these issues people have raised? How can we address them?'" Occasionally, a totally different course of action—a third way—emerges.

Of course, a monastery is not a Nasdaq company. "The decisions we make for our community affect our life, our home," Sister Noreen says. "They are about how we are going to live. It's not just about what we do from nine to five."

Are there drawbacks to doing business the monastic way? Certainly. The sisters agonized over what to do with the college's administration building through the tenures of four prioresses, over twenty years. Shareholders would have revolted long before that. But deliberating openly on significant decisions and deciding by consensus can create cohesiveness, whether it's in a monastic community or a tire manufacturing plant. These are practices to which many contemporary management gurus pay only lip service. Perhaps they need to spend some time in a monastery.

Prodigal Sons and Daughters

The story of the prodigal son may be the most familiar gospel parable. So familiar perhaps that it's easy to miss its nuanced layers. I might have missed them too if the Mount sisters hadn't focused on this parable at their annual retreat.

The story is the stuff of soap opera. A father has two sons: one who runs from his obligations, another who faithfully carries out his work. A crisis arises when the younger son's return home is greeted with celebration:

> The older brother became angry. When he refused to enter the house, his father came out and pleaded with him. The son said in reply, "All these years I served you and did not disobey your orders, yet you never gave me even a young goat to feast on with my friends. But when your son returns

who swallowed up your property with prostitutes, for him you slaughter the fattened calf."

The father said to him, "My son, you are here with me always; everything I own is yours. But now we must celebrate, because your brother was dead and has come to life again. He was lost and has been found."

As many times as I've heard the story, I've always identified with the dutiful older son. So it surprises me when the sisters praise the younger son's humility and willingness to repent. They suggest the angry older son is "walled off" from God. I feel like saying, "Listen, that son has a right to be indignant. The father is in denial, and the younger son is a self-centered jerk, and probably a phony too."

I might have kept that view if I hadn't begun, as the retreat leader suggested, to reframe the story and search for parts of myself in all three characters. Surely, there have been times when, like the younger son, I behaved so badly I needed to ask for forgiveness. Like the father, I've accepted a friend's or a relative's apology after a disagreement, encouraging them to "forget it and move on." More times than not, I've been like the older brother, so certain of my own convictions that I saw anyone who challenged them as hopelessly naive.

In fact, I've seen the dynamics of this parable play out all too often in our blended family. When I first married, my stepdaughters made it known they wanted my husband to visit them *alone*. As a newlywed, I interpreted this as an attempt to come between my husband and me. What I refused to admit was that I was hurt they didn't particularly want to be with me. Instead, I complained about the weekends my husband spent with either of his daughters. He would say, "You are the one I'm with every day. You are the one I'm going to spend the rest of my life with. It's only a few times a year that I visit my daughters." *My son, you are here with me always; everything I own is yours.*

When I get angry with my stepdaughters, it's usually because they aren't acting as I think they should. Translated, that means they aren't acting as *I* would. That's the crux of our current conflict. My younger stepdaughter is about to go off to graduate school in Michigan. She wants to buy a house or condo rather than rent for the time she'll be in school. She's asked my husband to give her the money for a down payment. We disagree whether this is a wise move. It's not at all clear to me (or my husband, for that matter) how she'll manage monthly mortgage payments on a teaching assistant's salary. With the real estate market in a free fall, will she be able to sell the home when she finishes school?

I tell him I'm not opposed to his *ever* helping his daughter buy a home, but I suggest it might make more sense to wait until she settles somewhere on a long-term basis. But I also know it's a foregone conclusion he'll do what she asks. We can't seem to discuss the subject without both of us exploding in anger.

When my husband and his former wife separated, my stepdaughter was in her senior year in high school. I'm sure she felt her parents had ruined what should have been a stellar year for her. A "betrayal" is how she once described the divorce to me. He has spent the last nine years trying to rebuild their relationship. Perhaps he fears that if he doesn't provide this financial help, his daughter will consider it another "betrayal."

With these raw emotions swirling, we set out on the six-hour drive to Michigan. I return to the chapter on humility in *The Rule of St. Benedict*. So much of it focuses on controlling the tongue. "For Scripture warns, 'In a flood of words, you will not avoid sinning. . . .' Speak gently . . . seriously . . . briefly and reasonably."

I find further reinforcement in the "Tools for Good Works" chapter: "You are not to act in anger or nurse a grudge. . . . Never give a hollow greeting or turn away when someone needs your love. . . . Day by day, remind yourself that you are going to die. Hour by hour, keep careful watch over all you do, aware that God's gaze is upon you, wherever you may be."

All of St. Benedict's good counsel evaporates within the first few hours of my setting foot in Michigan. My stepdaughter has picked out properties to view that are nearly double the price my husband has set as his threshold. When he tells her they are too expensive, she fixes on a condominium that is still $20,000 over his price range. My anxiety grows when she asks my husband to meet with her alone. Again, I feel pushed to the sidelines. I fall back on my trusted defense mechanism, which is to blow up at him. I wonder, *Where is* conversatio *in all this? Am I capable of only reading The Rule's words but not living them?*

I think of the parable's older son. At the retreat, one of the sisters said of that brother, "He's upset over a decision that was not his to make. He wants to hold on to his self-righteousness, even to the point of cutting himself off from his entire family. To me, that's the part that's wrong."

It occurs to me that I've reacted much the same way to many of my husband's decisions regarding his daughters. And though I mightn't agree with them, like the father's in the parable, they were his decisions to make.

St. Luke's Gospel doesn't reveal what ultimately transpires in the prodigal son's family. We don't know if the bitter son accepts his father's explanation, enters the house, and embraces his younger brother, feeling reassured that his father loves them both. We don't know if he remains estranged from his family. We're not told if the two brothers work side by side from then on and prosper or if the second son slips back into his dissolute ways. We can't even be sure the father's love remains resolute. We can only imagine. The sole ending we can write is the one we want for our own story.

"Send Your Soul Ahead"

There are times when I feel that I am carrying my anger around on my back like a knapsack full of stones. On the weekend after the house-hunting debacle with my stepdaughter, I return to the Mount, still wrestling to shed those stones. When I meet again with Sister Thomasita, she encourages me not to lose heart. "Remember, *conversatio* is the work of a lifetime. It's not something that happens all at once or overnight," she says.

She has a suggestion. "The next time you visit your stepdaughter, send your soul ahead of you. Ask your soul to be present with her so that when you do come together, you come with a different kind of readiness. What I think happens is that you get angry at a situation, and then you get angry at yourself. So the anger rises to the next level and gets stacked up inside of you to the point where you don't know what to do with it." I know that she is right.

Sister Thomasita urges me to explore more deeply just what it is I'm so angry about. "I think you'll find that beneath your anger is a deep hurt," she gently suggests.

I take her words to heart. I suspect it's going to require confronting some Dorian Gray facets of myself I'd rather not expose. I'd probably have to admit that my anxiety over my stepdaughter's condo isn't really about the possibility it might prove to be a bad investment. Money has never been a big motivator for me. A more likely cause is envy—envy that things seem to come so easily to my stepdaughter. I worked for seven years at the *Washington Post* before saving enough money to purchase a condominium. I certainly didn't ask my parents for help.

If I explore the true causes of my anger, as Sister Thomasita suggests, I'd have to confront an even uglier side of myself. What I want least to admit is that my stepdaughters stand out in bold relief as a reminder that my husband once had a life with another woman. They represent an unbreakable bond with his former wife. Not surprisingly, what lurks beneath my anger is a cesspool of envy, rivalry, and insecurity, the very emotions St. Benedict underscores in the chapter on humility.

At Mass this morning, the first reading is from St. Paul's letter to the Galatians: "Now the works of the flesh are . . . hatred, rivalry, jealousy, outbursts of fury, acts of selfishness . . . occasions of envy. . . . The fruits of the Spirit are love, joy, peace, patience, kindness, generosity, faithfulness, gentleness, self-control." I seem to have a long-standing relationship with "the works of the flesh." I'd like to get better acquainted with "the fruits of the Spirit."

Sister Thomasita proposes I talk with Sister Janelle Maes, a psychologist who teaches a class for novices on the "shadow" emotions of anger, guilt, and shame. Sister Janelle offers a measure of hope: Anger isn't necessarily all bad. It can serve a purpose as well.

"As a matter of fact, St. Francis de Sales is said to have had a terrible temper, and he's a saint!" she says, laughing. Anger races to our side like an EMT when we feel threatened, confront an injustice, or suffer an injury. "When you see that anger is interfering with your life, that's when it's time to start *thinking* differently. You have to make an intervention with your thoughts, and once that happens, your feelings will crossover too. The questions to ask yourself are 'Where is this anger coming from? Is this anger helping me?'"

There's no point in pretending the anger isn't there, she says. That does more harm than good. "We only find our true self through radical self-honesty. That involves recognizing aspects of our character we may wish were different but accepting them anyway." By accepting them, we befriend them. By befriending them, we can tame them, Sister Janelle contends. And in that lies hope of *conversatio*.

I realize there aren't going to be any methadone fixes for my addiction to anger, only the addict's slow slog of making it through one day at a time and recognizing those times when I need to send my soul ahead.

V.

The Interior Life

THE WOODCARVER

Khing, the master carver, made a bell stand of precious wood. When it was finished, all who saw it were astounded. They said it must be the work of spirits. The Prince of Lu asked the woodcarver, "What is your secret?"

Khing replied, "I am only a workman. When I began to think about what you commanded, I guarded my spirit and did not expend it on trifles. I fasted in order to set my heart at rest. After three days of fasting, I had forgotten gain and success. After five days, I had forgotten praise or criticism. After seven days, I had forgotten my body with all its limbs. All that might distract me from the work had vanished. I was collected in the single thought of the bell stand.

"Then I went to the forest to see the trees in their natural state. My collected thought, free of distraction, was able to see the hidden potential in one of the trees. All I had to do was to put forth my hand and begin. From this encounter came the work that you ascribe to the spirits."

—Wisdom Story
as told by Sister Lillian Harrington, "Pilgrim Minister"

The Art of Pausing

When I worked in London, a colleague of mine would clear his desk in midafternoon, pull out a porcelain tea service from a desk drawer, and pause for afternoon tea. Others in the office, including me, kept right on working. We had not yet learned the art of pausing.

A question that continues to haunt me is whether it's practical, even possible, to live as a contemplative outside of a monastic setting. A quote in *Benedictines* magazine grabs my attention: "The mysticism of everyday life is the deepest mysticism of all." The line is from a book called *Seven Sacred Pauses* by Macrina Wiederkehr, a Benedictine sister from Arkansas. In the racecourse of our day, we need to recharge the spirit, Wiederkehr says, in the same way we need to stop for fuel on a journey.

Monastics, of course, enjoy natural pauses within the rhythm of their day through the Liturgy of the Hours, the times of communal prayer. A friend of mine who grew up on an Air Force base recalls how soldiers and family members alike would stop and stand at attention at the appointed time each day as the national anthem played over a loudspeaker. It was their moment to pause.

These breathers are like "treasured anointings in the midst of our work," Weiderkehr writes. "We slowly begin to see the holiness of so many things that remain hidden when we choose to rush through the hours, striking tasks from our to-do lists." We should emulate the African bushmen, she suggests, who work as safari guides. They pause at regular intervals and sit quite still. The purpose is not solely to rest. They are waiting for their souls to catch up with them on the journey. In those moments, they remain silent and listen for the tapping of the heart.

The pause can be as brief as stopping to observe a flower bed or as simple as breathing attentively. "Breathe in gratitude and compassion for yourself; breathe out love and encouragement for your coworkers, friends, family members," Wiederkehr says. "Your pause may be an awakening stretch or sitting quietly and remembering your name. . . . Ask yourself: is it possible to be less busy and still productive? Is it possible to look at work as ministry rather than just a means of employment?"

The Mount's Sister Agnes Honz works as a licensed massage therapist. After teaching for twenty years, then working an additional twenty as a hospital chaplain, she earned certificates in Swedish massage and reflexology so that she could give massages at homeless shelters. Sister Agnes talks often of "the mind-body-soul connection." She has taught me to pause whenever my writing is going poorly. "Take a few moments to massage the head," she says. "Gets a better blood flow going. You'll be more wide awake and ready for fresh ideas." I've tried it. It works.

Throughout the day, Sister Agnes periodically places her hand over her heart. She tries to sense the heart's rhythm. "Rub the spot where your heart is," she says. "Let the heart know you care about it." It is her way of pausing.

Even people who live in monasteries can lose a sense of the sacred if they go woodenly about their work, Wiederkehr warns. "There is a deeper purpose behind every assigned task, a purpose that goes far beyond just completing the job. When I wash dishes in our community, I try to be purposely conscious of the fact that I am not washing dishes just to get them done. Getting finished ought not to be my goal. . . . If this is the case, then I miss the experience of washing the dishes." I love that idea because doing the dishes is one of my least favorite household tasks. I find I can transform the drudgery if I focus on the pleasant sound of running water, allow myself to feel satisfaction at wiping the pots and plates clean, recall the tastiness of the meal they represent and the companionship I enjoyed at the table. "Realize that you are an artist," Wiederkehr says, whatever work you do.

"We tend to think of the work of creation as something completed," the paleontologist and Jesuit philosopher Pierre Teilhard de Chardin once said, "but that would be quite wrong." The work of creation is always unfolding. We serve to complete it, he said, "with the work of our hands."

Perhaps the dissatisfaction I've felt lately in my professional life stems from losing sight of my work as a continuation of creation. I haven't paused long enough to search for the mysteries in each day, whether I'm at the monastery or on my job. *The mysticism of everyday life is the deepest mysticism of all.*

Living Inside of a Paradox

It is beginning to dawn on me that to live a contemplative life is to dwell in the heart of paradox.

Here, at the monastery, individuals reject personal wealth but share in the pooled assets of the community.

From its perch on a hill, Mount St. Scholastica Monastery's distinctive red brick facade towers over the city of Atchison.

St. Scholastica Chapel was dedicated in 1938 during the monastery's 75th jubilee.

Detail of St. Benedict and St. Scholastica from a window in the choir chapel at Mount St. Scholastica that features Emil Frei's Atchison-blue stained glass.

Detail from an Emil Frei Atchison-blue stained glass window showing the Benedictine saints Walburga, Hildegard of Bingen, and Gertrude, surrounded by the words *Nos pariter ad vitam aeternam perducat* (May He lead us to everlasting life).

This choir chapel window is an image of of St. Benedict and includes a quotation from The Rule that inspired the author to begin her journey with the Mount sisters: *Omni tempore silentio debent studere* (At all times cultivate silence).

The Mount community's *schola*, or small choir, sings at Sunday Mass under the direction of Sister Irene Nowell.

The Mount sisters gather four times a day to pray the Liturgy of the Hours: Morning Praise, Mid-day Prayer, Evening Praise, and Compline.

Sister Elizabeth Carillo prays the words of the ancient Suscipe (Receive me, O Lord, as you have promised that I may live; disappoint me not in my hope) at her final profession of vows on the Feast of the Epiphany, January 2011.

Sister Lillian Harrington, the monastery's "Pilgrim Minister," who encouraged the author to "think about living."

Sister Thomasita Homan, who introduced the author to the Mount community and served as her "monastic guide."

Prioress Sister Anne Shepard (at right) blesses the Mount sisters each August as they begin a new season of ministry. Also pictured are Sisters Maria Nguyen, Susan Holmes and Bridget Dickason (right to left).

The Benedictine ring worn by the Mount sisters signifying their lifelong commitment to the monastic community.

Here, women forgo a marriage partner but have companions for life, companions who will sit at their bedside even as they die. It's something I, as a married woman without children, can only hope to have.

Here, women sacrifice the opportunity for childbearing, yet they are loved by hundreds of former students whose lives they helped guide.

Here, prayer involves not only words but—in equal measure—silence.

Here, one seeks God not simply through dogma, sacrament, or study, but through what the author William H. Shannon calls "the darkness of unknowing."

In a book called *Thomas Merton's Dark Path: The Inner Experience of a Contemplative*, Shannon writes, "The time has come to go beyond concepts into the dark but truer knowledge of God that lies beyond. This is the call to move from knowing God with clear concepts to knowing God in the darkness of 'unknowing.' We . . . plunge with abandon into the Darkness of Pure Faith."

St. John of the Cross described the contemplative life in similarly paradoxical terms:

> In order to have pleasure in everything
> Desire to have pleasure in nothing.
> In order to arrive at possessing everything
> Desire to possess nothing.
> In order to arrive at being everything
> Desire to be nothing.
> In order to arrive at knowing everything
> Desire to know nothing.

The notion of paradox emerges too in the readings for this Sunday's Mass. In a letter to the Corinthians, Paul complains of suffering as a "sting in the flesh." He doesn't say what that "sting" is. Anger, anxiety, physical pain, loneliness? (Fill in the blank.) He does say, "Three times I begged the Lord about this, that it might leave me." Eventually, Paul arrives at an insight: He can alter the way he *thinks* about his defect. "Therefore I am content with weaknesses, insults, hardships, persecutions, and constraints," he says. "For when I am weak, then I am strong."

The gospel reading from Mark recounts a rare moment in Jesus' ministry. He returns to his hometown of Nazareth, hoping to preach and to heal. But the attitude of the people seems to stymie him. Mark writes, "He was not able to perform any mighty deed there, apart from curing a few sick people by laying his hands on them. He was amazed at their lack of faith."

In his homily, Abbot Owen Purcell considers the letter to the Corinthians, and offers this paraphrase of St. Paul's words: "Our *incompletion* is our dignity, and when we feel it, we are most truly ourselves. . . . The cracks in our lives are what let in light." We too can "stifle" Jesus, he adds, "if we retain a self-defeating frame of mind that says, 'When I am weak, then I am embarrassed. I glory only in being able to look good and feel good all on my own.'"

The life of contemplation, Thomas Merton often said, entails a slow uncovering of the "true self." I read incessantly, take workshops, and periodically go into therapy or receive spiritual direction all out of a desire to know the true self. And yet, I waste so much time stifling that self, hiding my defects so that the face I show the world will not appear flawed. "We are at liberty to be real, or to be unreal," Merton writes in *New Seeds of Contemplation*. "We may wear one mask and now another." But if we chose the way of falseness, he says, "we must not be surprised that truth eludes us when we finally come to need it!"

Abbot Owen ends his homily with some lines from the Sufi poet Rumi: "Your defects are the way that glory is manifested. Don't turn your head, keep looking at the bandaged place. That is where the light enters you." I vow to keep my eye on those bandaged places.

Details

Today at Morning Praise, I notice some wax drippings have run down the sides of the candle that sits in the middle of the choir chapel. The candle is an integral part of community prayers. It is lit just before prayers begin. When it is extinguished, that is the signal to close our Psalters and store them in their little alcoves until it is time to gather again. The wax drippings catch my eye because I've never seen anything in the chapel look untidy, not so much as a mite of dust in the corners of the floor.

In the fifteen-minute break between Morning Praise and the beginning of Mass, I leave to get a cup of tea. When I return, the wax has been shaved from the side of the candle. It looks good as new. The drippings had not escaped the eagle eye of Sister Rosemary Bertels, the sacristan who keeps the flowers fresh, the pews dusted, the scripture books open to the right pages, and the altar cloths cleaned and starched.

I thought about how much attention the sisters pay to detail. For "feast days"—days that honor a particular saint or a major event in the life of Christ—a more elaborate bouquet of flowers might sit in front of the lectern. Instead of a bare altar, a series of potted plants might decorate the space, and a colored cloth might hang as a backdrop—white and gold for the Feast of the Body and Blood of Christ or white and red for a feast day honoring a Christian martyr. It is like walking into a well-appointed home where every piece of furniture, picture on a wall, or table decoration fit seamlessly together.

"Regard all utensils and goods of the monastery as sacred vessels of the altar, aware that nothing is to be neglected," St. Benedict writes in *The Rule*. Here, neatness connotes reverence. Objects last for decades because "nothing is to be neglected." When I see the beauty it creates at the monastery, I want to replicate a similar respect for everyday objects in my own home—not just my grandmother's china or my prized, signed poetry books, but everything from the tea kettle to the soap dish. I can't help thinking if I take better care of the things around me, if I reverence the "small" things, I'm apt to take better care of the people nearby too.

Counting Costs

At dinner one evening, Sister Anne, the prioress, announces that a nearby Catholic college has received $750,000 from a private donor to construct a grotto in honor of the Virgin Mary. Back in my room, I research what the same amount of money could buy: 750 freshwater wells in Africa, seven

Habitat for Humanity townhouses, food for a family of four for a dozen years.

A grotto for the Mount is also in the works. Sister Anne called a friend whose husband is a bricklayer. She told him, "I've got the bricks, and I've got a statue of the Blessed Mother." The bricklayer agreed to do the work for free. The Mount will get its grotto. And it won't cost the equivalent of twelve years' tuition at Harvard.

Some Prayers in the Game Room

When the storm sirens sound, I am sitting on a bench outside the Mount's guest quarters, hoping to witness my first Kansas tornado. I had slept through a microburst a few nights ago, so this time I dash outside at the sight of pebble-sized hail and some pitchfork lightning in the northeast sky. But as soon as the tornado siren sounds, Bill Caylor, one of the Mount's maintenance engineers, rushes over and orders me inside. He has been getting updates on the path of the storm via cell phone from his wife who is home watching the TV. Thick, slate-colored clouds crowd the sky, and the air feels dense as pudding. In the midst of it, Sister Anne drives by in her car, waves to Bill and me, and says she's off to get a haircut.

"The sisters have no fear," Bill says, shaking his head.

By the time Bill and I get inside, the sisters are already making their way down stairwells to the tornado shelter in what is euphemistically called the "game room." Some second-hand exercise equipment is stored there. The only game-related objects seem to be a threadbare pool table and a dilapidated ping-pong table. Luckily, the tornado isn't moving quickly.

Many of the older sisters are still making their way to the basement a full fifteen minutes after the siren has sounded.

The room is furnished with stuffing-deprived sofas and wicker chairs that look like antiques. The sisters arrange folding chairs so that people can sit and face one another and have a nice chat despite the tornado threat. They've been through this drill before and remain remarkably calm. Sister Eleanor Suther, the director of the Mount's retreat center, casually flips through the pages of a sewing magazine. Sister Johnette Putnam tries to get a pool game going. Sister Trinitas Miles fingers a rosary, silently mouthing the prayers. Sister Lucille Borengasser, just back from visiting inmates at the jail, complains the evacuation has cut short her afternoon nap. She slips into one of the easy chairs, saying she'll just have to nap there.

Sister Mary Liz Schweiger, the subprioress, has been receiving weather updates by phone. She announces a tornado has been spotted in the area and suggests the sisters pray "for the people of Atchison." The chatting stops. The sisters pray aloud, "Remember, oh most gracious Virgin Mary, that never was it known that anyone who fled to your protection, implored your help, or sought your intercession was left unaided. . . ." They pray the Our Father and the Hail Mary. Sister Mary Liz then suggests they continue to pray in silence. A few moments pass. Then the faint, shaky voice of one of the elderly sisters breaks the silence. She begins to sing, "Immaculate Mary, your praises we sing. . . ." Soon the whole room joins in.

It suddenly strikes me that the sisters aren't praying for their own safety. They're praying for everyone else's.

I have the distinct feeling I am not going to die today. But the thought does cross my mind that if I have to die somewhere, I'd rather it be at the Mount than anywhere else. There's no one besides my husband with whom I'd rather be.

Soon Sister Mary Liz gets a call on her cell phone. The storm has passed north of the monastery and is unlikely to return. The chairs go back to their original positions. Everyone files out, as if a party has come to an abrupt end.

Later in the day, word gets around that Sister Anne made it to the hairdresser's. The tornado warning had interrupted her shampoo. But, she says, she still managed to get a pretty good cut and style.

Fourth of July

Some people like to sleep later on holidays. I never did. I've always wanted to make the most of the days that are mine to do with as I please. At the monastery, I find myself rising even earlier than usual. The predawn hours arrive with their breakfast tray full of fresh ideas. The most wonderful moment of the day, Thomas Merton once wrote, "is that moment when creation in its innocence asks permission to 'be' once again, as it did on that first morning that ever was."

I decide to explore the neighborhood around the monastery, something I haven't had time to do on previous visits. Once, the sisters lived alone on their hill. Now, a hodgepodge of houses surrounds them. A newly renovated brick rambler with brass horseshoe knockers stands on one side of the street. Next to it: A house with worn siding rests unevenly on a concrete slab. Neighbors chat porch to porch. A young man rides an all-terrain vehicle up and down Seventh Street. Teenagers shoot off firecrackers and cherry bombs, though it isn't even noon yet.

I wonder if we would sing patriotic songs at community prayers. At a parish I attended in Chicago, men wearing Revolutionary War costumes would march up the main aisle at the start of Mass, carrying the American flag. America may be the one country on earth where national identity attaches itself to a sense of divine purpose. *America, America, God shed his grace on thee.*

In chapel, however, we do not sing any of the traditional "hymns" to America. For the national holiday, we sing what is probably far more appropriate for a national holiday, "The Prayer of St. Francis":

> Lord, make me a means of your peace,
> where there is hatred grown, let me sow your love
> where there is injury, Lord,
> let forgiveness be my sword.

As a recessional, Sister Janelle plays "My Country 'Tis of Thee" on the organ, but no one belts out the words. I do not think this is because the sisters are unpatriotic, nor do I think they don't love and bless this country. But to be a monastic is to live as a citizen of the world. It requires love for every country on the planet. In that context, a prayer for peace *is* the only anthem worth singing.

Prayer, Presence, and Insights at the Amtrak Station

I can probably count on one hand the times I have failed to attend the community prayers at the Mount. There are nights I go to bed so exhausted that I think, *There is no way I'm going to make it to Morning Praise at 6:30.* Then the alarm rings at 5:30, and I bolt out of bed. I would miss too much the distinctive sound of those women's voices, singing as one.

Even though I love the prayers, I often feel as if I'm missing something essential. Some of the sisters sit with their eyes closed. Others stare, as if they're thoroughly taken up with prayer . . . or so I imagine them to be.

My mind, on the other hand, sprints from thought to thought. I sing the words of the Psalm on the page in front of me, but mentally I'm reworking the last paragraph I wrote before dashing over to chapel. I might revisit a conversation, or enumerate what I need to buy from Wal-Mart. Some phrase from the Psalm usually draws me back. I focus on it for a few moments, but then the mind is off again. Simone Weil once called prayer "an intense form of paying attention." I wondered why I couldn't attain the same attitude of attentiveness I sensed among the sisters.

Then something changed. We were reading Psalm 15:

> Whoever walks without blame, doing what is right.
> Speaking truth from the heart,
> Who does not slander a neighbor,
> Does no harm to another,
> Never defames a friend,
> Who disdains the wicked

> But honors those who fear the Lord,
> Who keeps an oath despite the cost,
> Lends no money at interest,
> Accepts no bribe against the innocent,
> Whoever acts like this will not be shaken. . . .

Suddenly, I felt the rest of the room slip away. I became aware of only the words on the page before me and the sound of the sisters' voices. It was as if the Psalm's words were entering me and I them. I didn't have to work at paying attention. I wondered, *If I can feel these words so intensely, maybe, just maybe, when I walk outside this chapel, I can live them as well.*

A former monk of the Abbey of Gethsemani tells a story about entering the abbey church one evening and finding Thomas Merton on his knees. Merton was so absorbed in prayer, he was completely oblivious to the fact that anyone else was nearby. Merton ultimately rejected the notion of prayer as something to be "worked at." He saw it instead as a kind of "presence." In that instant, the pray-er becomes the prayer. Perhaps, in some rudimentary way, that is what I experienced in chapel.

I wish I could say the experience repeated itself and that I had ascended to a higher promontory in my prayer practice. But whenever I return home, I struggle to keep a discipline of praying the Liturgy of the Hours. I miss the poetry of the sisters' translation of Psalms. Another huge difference: The community isn't there. I lack the energy that's unleashed when those voices pray together as one.

Even more problematic is my erratic schedule. Sometimes I have to dash out the door at 6:30 a.m. to catch a plane. No time then to sit quietly and pray Morning Praise. When I'm on an out-of-town assignment, work often drags on until late in the evening. Evening Praise might well turn into midnight prayer. With some reluctance, I've had to admit the kind of work I do probably won't ever permit me to sit and meditate in the same chair at the same time every day. But I wondered, *What kind of prayer* could *I do?*

An "answer" of sorts came to me one sultry July afternoon. It had been a travel day from hell. I started out at 6:00 a.m., driving in a rental car from Washington, DC, to Baltimore–Washington International Airport. Landing in Chicago two hours later, I grabbed my rolling suitcase and dashed to the elevated train that would take me to the Amtrak station downtown. After a two-and-a-half-hour train ride, I'd be home.

Chicago's Union Station was even more of a madhouse than usual that day. About fifty people stood ahead of me in the ticket line. There were only four agents on duty—one of them a trainee whose transactions took twice as long to complete. To boot, the air conditioning had conked out. All this whipped up a good sweat in the passengers, not to mention a foul mood. A woman with a T-shirt that said *Don't tread on me* yelled at the agents to get the line moving, which was followed by disgruntled murmurs from others of "This is ridiculous!" and "These people are idiots!"

I felt myself getting swept up in the anger. Then I paused. I said a silent prayer for the "Don't-tread-on-me" woman and for the overwhelmed ticket agents. I realized my prayer could involve more than keeping myself calm and centered. I could smile at the furious, frustrated passengers; chat a moment with two bewildered-looking teenage girls; lend a hand to a family overloaded with baggage. Sister Imogene Baker's definition of contemplation returned to me: "Be where you are, and do what you're doing." I could surrender to the moment, prayerfully—"mindfully" the Buddhists might say. And with that surrender came a sense of peace.

To be sure, I still engage in prayers of petition. I regularly deliver my "wish list" to God. Please heal my brother-in-law, Herb, of cancer. Please help my cousin Pat, who is suffering with early onset Alzheimer's. Please let me do a good job today. But praying has become less a matter of putting my quarter in the dispensing machine and expecting the gumballs to roll out. Some mornings, the only conscious prayer I can muster is to sing the refrain of one of my favorite invitatory hymns at Morning Praise: "As morning breaks, I look to you. I look to you, Oh Lord, to be my strength this day, as morning breaks, as morning breaks." I sing it silently to myself or out loud if no one else is around.

Sometimes all I can come up with during the course of a busy work day are these lines from one of the evening hymns I love: "God of all be praised. Be forever praised."

Increasingly, though, I've come to view prayer as the seam that runs through every part of my day. Exercising at the gym, I look upon my routines as a form of prayer—a chance to express gratitude for a body that, in midlife, can still perform lunges, squats, and sit-ups (well, most of the time). When I drive to Chicago for work, the two-and-a-half-hour commute turns into a meditation. I pray for the safety of the drivers weaving in and out of lanes; for the farmers whose crops of corn and soybeans I pass along Interstate 55; for the people living in the wood-frame houses of Lexington, Pontiac, Odell, and the other small towns I pass. When I walk with my husband in our neighborhood in the morning before we set off for work, our walks become a meditation, too. Prayer no longer represents separate moments in my day. It is the day itself.

There are days, though, when my actions resemble anything but prayer. Like the time, at another Amtrak station, I argued so vociferously with a ticket agent who refused to give me the refund I was due that the police arrived! Those are the times I have to remind myself of Sister Thomasita's definition of *conversatio* as a constant conversation with life. It's less about doing the right thing every time than it is about muddling through.

An anonymous Zen master once wrote about prayer as I am coming to understand it:

> I see a person riding on an ox, looking for an ox,
> searching for what isn't lost,
> climbing an invisible mountain,
> striving for what is already possessed,
> dividing people in order to unite,
> killing to achieve peace,
> working for grace, which is a gift,
> alienating to bring people together,
> questing for God while already standing on holy ground.

VI.

Conversatio/The Constant Turning

A Young Monk and His Elder

A young monk approached one of his elders and said, "Try as I might to be good-tempered, chaste, and sober, I keep on sinning. Therefore, I am not suited to the monastic life."

The older monk replied, "Brother, the spiritual life is this: I rise and I fall, I rise and I fall."

The young monk stayed and persevered.

—Wisdom Story
from *The Sayings of the Desert Fathers and Mothers*,
as told by Sister Lillian Harrington, "Pilgrim Minister"

A Death at the Mount

The Mount in mid-autumn is a study in splendor. The feather reed grass stands tall, each blade like a long stylus swaying in the wind. The cooler weather paints the trees on the Missouri River bluffs into an artist's palette. Bright maroon cockscombs rise like balls of fire in the drying grasses. The air is crisp and fragrant with the smell of wet leaves and wood burning.

This time, I return to the Mount in a professional capacity to report a segment for PBS-TV on contemporary monastic life. The producer assigned to work with me is the same one with whom I had a bitter blowup a year ago. We have worked together only a few times since our conflict. Now, he'll be visiting my beloved Mount. I guess this is a case of what Sister Thomasita would call "God's unerring sense of humor."

I am a little apprehensive. He has a producer's tendency to demand things NOW. Will he offend the sisters? What if we have another flare-up? But when my producer walks through the door at 7:45 on the first morning of the shoot, and Sister Thomasita and I are there to meet him, he is wearing a wide grin. "I've sent the cameraman ahead to take some shots of the grounds. The light this morning is just *perfect!*" he announces. The forecast had called for rain. Instead, sunlight strokes the treetops and falls like a spotlight on the turning leaves. I start to feel as if the taping for our story just might go "perfectly" too.

There is a parallel story playing out in the life of the monastery—one that will form a subplot to my PBS segment. A sister is dying. The previous evening, community members began "sitting with" Sister Phyllis Dye. Whenever a community member is dying, the sisters keep a twenty-four hour vigil at her bedside. I remember Sister Phyllis from the night shift I spent at the monastery's nursing care wing. Frozen in dementia, she wouldn't—or couldn't—respond when spoken to. She refused to take her medication. It was as if she had expended her last coins on life and wasn't about to throw any more good money after bad.

A few days after my evening in the nursing center, I was shopping in the monastery gift shop. A photograph on the front of a greeting card caught my eye. The photographer had captured the precise moment in a sunset when the sky turns from mango to berry blue. Mottled clouds hovered over a black, mysterious shoreline. It was a photograph of considerable artistic depth. I flipped the card over. On the backside it said, *Photo by Phyllis Dye, O.S.B.*

I bought it. Later, Sister Thomasita told me Sister Phyllis adored fishing and probably snapped the picture on a boating trip. For reasons I didn't quite understand, every time I came to the Mount for months afterward, I kept Sister Phyllis's photograph displayed on my writing desk. It was difficult to reconcile my impression of the vibrant, keen-eyed photographer who captured that sunset with the shell of a woman I'd seen in the nursing care wing.

During a break in the taping, Sister Anne (the prioress) and Sister Thomasita accompany me to Sister Phyllis's bedside. She wears a flowered nightgown and looks as if she has shrunk several sizes since the last time I saw her. She lies on her side. A stamp-size scapular of brown cloth with an image of Jesus' heart is draped across her chest. I ask about the scapular. "We wear them to remind us of God's protection, especially in the hour of death," Sister Thomasita says. The nurses have placed a moist washcloth over Sister Phyllis's forehead. Oxygen tubes extend from her nostrils. The breathing mechanism makes a metronomic *tss tss* sound that competes with the low gurgle of Sister Phyllis's breathing. Her chest barely moves with each breath. I have never been with anyone who is this close to death. My parents both died suddenly in cities where I was not living at the time. So this, I gather, is what dying looks like.

"There's going to be great fishing in heaven," Sister Thomasita whispers, taking Sister Phyllis's hand.

The prioress touches Sister Phyllis's arm. "Mottling is setting in," she says loudly enough that I'm sure Sister Phyllis can hear her. It means Sister Phyllis's blood flow is slowing. The skin of her hands and feet are turning a brownish-yellow color. "They'll be no more pain when you get to heaven," Sister Anne says.

"The sooner the better," another sister, who has been keeping the bedside vigil for the past hour, chimes in.

I'm thinking, *Why are they saying these things? If hearing is the last sense to go, then she probably can hear all this. Why don't they tell her to keep fighting, to hold on to life?*

Together, the sisters pray an Our Father. I do not join in. Occasionally, Sister Phyllis grimaces. When she opens her eyes, they appear moist. Is it possible she's weeping because she's moved by the prayers, or because she realizes she's dying? Perhaps she isn't crying at all.

❧

Our PBS shoot goes smoothly. Sister Anne and Sister Thomasita invite my producer to eat breakfast with them on our last day of taping. He protests that he doesn't like to eat while he's working. Then he proceeds to consume two soft-boiled eggs along with a bran muffin the kitchen baked from scratch that morning.

Later, when we finish taping an interview with one of the sisters who works as a clinical social worker, my producer takes her aside. The cameraman and I overhear him telling her about his difficult divorce and that he'd like to be a more spiritual person. We look at each other stupefied. It isn't at all like this producer to reveal details of his personal life, especially not to anyone we're interviewing for a story. But around here, his actions aren't all that strange. The Mount works its magic in myriad ways on the people who come here. My producer probably is just living out his *conversatio,* like the rest of us are trying to live ours.

I check in again on Sister Phyllis the following day. For years, she took care of a stray cat called Ebony. Today, the nurses lay Callie, another of the cats, at the foot of Sister Phyllis's bed. (Ebony was deemed too wild to be let inside.) Sister Phyllis's breathing has become more labored. The nursing staff counts only six breaths a minute, followed by forty-five seconds of apnea, or not breathing. Somehow Sister Phyllis manages to keep a faint hold on life. "I was with Sister Phyllis when her father was dying," one of the sisters who works at the Mount's nursing care center says. "He went the same way, holding on. You wonder why."

At a quarter to five the next morning, the phone rings in my room. It is Sister Anne informing me that Sister Phyllis had died just fifteen minutes before. She invites me to pay my respects. I wonder what it will be like to see someone who has been dead for only a matter of minutes. I wonder if the sisters will be overcome with emotion.

Sister Phyllis is lying face up on her bed in a paisley nightgown. The cloth square of her scapular still lies on her chest. Her eyelids are not quite closed. She looks like someone who has drifted into the first moments of sleep. Her lips are parted ever so slightly, and I can see some silver bridgework on her bottom left molars.

But what a stunning transformation! Her body lies perfectly at ease. Her skin looks practically luminous. Her face, no longer grimaced in pain, is as smooth as a much younger woman's. The room is so quiet I can hear my own breathing. The quietness of death. *Dying is ugly,* I think, *but death, death has a certain beauty.* It reminds me of how one season spills into another, often imperceptibly. Death, in that context, seems to flow naturally from life, like the crossing from the womb into this world.

Sister Mary Liz, the subprioress, arrives to make sure Sister Phyllis's clothing, eyeglasses, and Rosary will be ready when the undertakers come.

"Are you wearing your ring, Phyllis?" Sister Mary Liz asks, gently lifting the stiff left hand from beneath a blanket to see if Sister Phyllis is wearing the Benedictine ring she received the day she took her final vows. The nurses have removed it.

"Death is such a mystery," Sister Mary Liz says. "As many sisters as we've seen die over the years, we still really don't know what takes place. When my mother was dying, my sister Martha and I were with her. But I have another sister who was coming in from California. We didn't know if she would get there in time. So my sister said, 'Tell her even if I'm not there yet, it's okay to go. She doesn't have to wait for me. If she can get into heaven one minute sooner, she should do it.' So I said that to my mother. Now, my mother had been hard of hearing since the age of eighteen, but not twenty minutes after I had said that, she died." Sister Mary Liz's eyes fill with tears. "In that moment, I believe my mother could hear again."

Sister Mary Liz says that some sisters die peacefully, and some struggle quite a bit. "One kept stretching her hands out in front of her, for whatever reason. Another would make the Sign of the Cross and bless every person who came into the room."

One by one, as news of Sister Phyllis's death spreads, sisters stream into the room. "She's the first one of our class to go," says Sister Bernelda Nanneman, a compact woman with a shock of short white hair.

"Whenever she came home with me, she'd say, 'Tell your mother to make that chopped suey stuff,'" recalls Sister Rosemary Bertels, another of her classmates.

Sister Dolores Wagner, normally one of the quietest sisters in the monastery, rushes over to the bedside and exclaims, "Oh, dear Phyllis!" She kisses Sister Phyllis on the cheek.

No one chokes up. Except me. I'm so moved by the affection the sisters show for their friend. Even after all these months of getting to know the sisters, I hate to be seen crying in front of them. I thank them for letting me share in this moment with the community, and I quickly leave before anyone sees my tears.

In chapel that morning, we sing the words of Psalm 1: "Happy are they who hope in the Lord." I think of Sister Phyllis.

A portrait of Sister Phyllis's life begins to emerge, in stages, the way a photographic image grows gradually sharper in a basin of darkroom chemicals. Sister Phyllis wasn't a scholar or a sought-after speaker. She taught reading to schoolchildren across Kansas and Missouri. And when she retired, she asked to return home to the monastery to do "quiet, plain work." She tended the gardens, made flower arrangements for the dining room tables, and preserved fruits and vegetables in the canning house. Quiet, plain work.

An infant brother had died before she was born, and then her mother died when she was still quite young. Her father, who served in the military, frequently left her in the care of relatives. Though her family was Baptist, she attended the boarding school the sisters ran at the Mount. With what must have taken considerable courage, she informed her relatives in her sophomore year of college that she was converting to Catholicism. Two years later, she entered the Benedictine order.

Additional details emerge in a book written by Sister Phyllis's cousin, Ann Hyman, a journalist from Florida. The two were close as children, and Sister Phyllis briefly lived with Hyman's family. Then they lost touch for many years. But one summer in the mid-1990s, on a kind of journey through her heritage, Hyman decided to visit her cousin in the Benedictine monastery. She expected Sister Phyllis to resemble the nuns in *The Bells of St. Mary's*. The person she found was more like Huck Finn. Sister Phyllis took Hyman fishing in Hannibal, on the Mississippi. Driving past tall rows of ripening corn, she whispered to Hyman, "If you stand quietly in the middle of a field, you can hear the corn grow."

Even with Sister Phyllis's death, business at the monastery goes on as usual. Sister Elena Hernandez, who is from Mexico, spends the day with her *parakeeta* Tina, who has pneumonia and can't fly, periodically feeding Tina her medicine from an eyedropper. Some of the sisters participate in a marathon to raise money for cancer research. Others watch a DVD of the dog flick *Marley & Me*.

When my mother died, I couldn't think of anything but the funeral we were planning. I didn't want to talk. The sound of anyone's laughter offended me. My mother died two days before the terrorist attacks in 2001. While the rest of the nation remained transfixed in front of the TV, I watched next to nothing of the news coverage. I was locked in my personal shell of shock and grief. The routine of these days at the Mount surprises and puzzles me. "Death doesn't subtract a sister from the community," Sister Thomasita tells me. "It just means one more sister has extended our community into eternity."

In the afternoon, I spot Sister Kathleen Egan in one of the lounge areas. She is watching the news about the Nobel Peace Prize winners on TV. She looks sturdier, more alert than she did on my last visit.

I ask her what she's been up to lately. "People ask me what I do with my days, and I say, 'It doesn't matter what I do. Everyday is wonderful because I don't have many more left. I love every day because it might be my last.'" She interrupts herself and says, "Look at those lovely roses." She points to a garden outside the nursing care center's floor-to-ceiling windows. "Look at that tall one! Can you see it?" My eyes follow her finger to a single red bloom. "I don't think I've ever seen more beautiful roses than the ones this year," she says.

Sister Kathleen recounts a theory she has. It is that our lives on earth are merely an interlude. "That's not to denigrate this life," she emphasizes. "This life is a gift. But it's a gift we're given between the life we left when we were born and the life we're returning to."

Tomorrow, the monastery will receive back the body of Sister Phyllis. There will be an evening prayer service, the first in a series of steps commending her to the next life—the one to which, Sister Kathleen reminds me, we are all returning.

When the silver hearse carrying Sister Phyllis's coffin arrives at the monastery entrance, the sisters line up to meet it. The day is overcast, and a fine mist is falling. The yellow leaves of a

Cleveland pear tree just outside the doorway shine like patches of light in the mist. Two undertakers in gray suits wheel in the coffin. It is a simple silver aluminum casket. Outside, the bells begin to toll. I think of the neighbors accustomed to hearing these bells call the sisters to morning and evening prayer. I wonder if, after all these years, they know that bells in midafternoon signify the loss of another community member.

The sisters stand at attention. Sister Anne sprinkles the casket with a fern branch she has dipped in holy water. One of Sister Phyllis's classmates stands by, holding a framed copy of the handwritten vows Sister Phyllis signed on January 1, 1956, the day she became a permanent member of the community. I have only seen the dead received with such dignity at official state funerals or military ceremonies at Arlington National Cemetery. Steadying herself on a cane, another sister reads from Sister Phyllis's worn copy of *The Rule of St. Benedict*. "Never swerving from his instructions, then, but faithfully observing his teaching in the monastery until death, we shall through patience share in the sufferings of Christ that we may deserve also to share in his kingdom. . . ." I think about the day I might have to stand in this entranceway to say goodbye to my friend and mentor, Sister Thomasita. Or to Sister Lillian, Sister Kathleen, or any of the many other community members I've come to love. And then I struggle again not to cry.

We march two by two with the casket to St. Lucy's Chapel in the Dooley Center, where Sister Phyllis attended daily Mass in the last years of her life. The high, wrap-around windows look out on a layer of gray stratus clouds. Sister Phyllis's casket is placed beside the altar, between portraits of St. Benedict and St. Scholastica. The sisters display *The Rule* on a stand. On a side table, in front of a large white candle, they set down the vows signed more than fifty years ago on specially treated paper that won't crumble or fade.

The first prayer is the *Suscipe*, the same one Sister Phyllis spoke when she professed her final vows: "Receive me, O Lord, as you have promised, that I may live. Disappoint me not in my hope." It has all come full circle now. We recite the Midday Psalms. The Liturgy of the Hours, after all, must go on. Then, in silence, we walk two by two to the casket to pay our respects.

When I look inside the coffin, I can hardly believe my eyes. The person lying there, wearing a black blazer and a white blouse, looks not at all like the woman I saw a few days ago, moments after her death. That woman was peaceful, almost radiant. The body in the casket seems like nothing more than clay: hard and dull.

I remembered something my mother's undertaker had told me after her wake. I had interviewed Whit Sloane for a series on Chicago Public Radio called *In Search of the Soul.* Sloane had said, "This work brings you to a clear understanding that there is something beyond this life. As undertakers, we are agents of change, of that transfer, that crossing over. We are servants of a great mystery. I don't know any funeral directors or embalmers who don't believe there is something more than the body, who don't believe in the soul."

When I asked him what was the most significant thing he had learned about death, he said it is as if the body's "essential spark" has been extinguished. All that remains is "organic matter." I didn't know then what he meant. After seeing the difference between Sister Phyllis today and moments after her death, I think I know.

We leave the chapel in silence. Most of the sisters disperse to their rooms, though a few remain behind to sit with the casket. Back in my room, I stare out the window at the evergreens and elm trees. Yesterday, I hadn't noticed them. Four squirrels briskly chase one another. I feel grateful to still be among the living, an inhabitant of this world Sister Kathleen calls an "interlude" between two destinations. I think of a poem by Li-Young Lee, called "The Hammock," in which Lee observes that we live between two great unknowns ("Is it a door, and goodbye on either side?" the poet asks). And what this life amounts to, he says, is "a little singing between two great rests."

The day of Sister Phyllis's funeral, a fine mist falls. Dull light seeps through the chapel windows, their Atchison blue seeming deeper, more somber. The deep maroon of the cockscombs in a vase near the altar offers a welcome splash of color.

The choir sings:

> I know that my Redeemer lives
> and on the last day I shall rise again.
> In my body I shall look on God my Savior.
> I myself shall see him.
> Mine own eyes shall gaze on him.
> In my body I shall look on God my Savior.

This is the hope I cherish in my heart.

They sing with such conviction, "I *know* that my Redeemer lives." Perhaps they sing to convince those of us who fear and doubt.

As a novice, Sister Bridget Dickason worked in the monastery gardens with Sister Phyllis. When their work was done, the two sometimes went fishing. "Phyllis helped me learn how to balance monastic life, prayer, work, and leisure," Sister Bridget says. "She was faithful to the Liturgy of the Hours and the Eucharist. However, if the fish were biting and it was time for Vespers [here she mimics holding a fishing rod], we prayed with extended arms: our poles raised high in supplication for a keeper." Everyone laughs.

In the day's gospel reading, Jesus knows he will soon have to leave his disciples, and he prays, "I wish that where I am, they may also be." For most of her life, Sister Bridget explains, Sister Phyllis could not be with many of the people she loved: her mother who had died, her father who was often away, the relatives she left behind when she entered the Benedictines. "Death is the price we pay to be reunited with those who have gone before us in faith," Sister Bridget says. *Yes,* I think, *but a pretty steep price to pay.*

At the end of the service, we grab our coats and step out into the chill morning to walk behind the casket to the cemetery. Two gravediggers wait at the top of a hill. Their ample bellies flow over their dungarees; their hooded red sweatshirts blaze under the gray sky. These are the real grim reapers, not at all like the pale, emaciated chess master in Ingmar Bergman's

The Seventh Seal. They are waiting for Sister Phyllis, and—in a sense—for us all.

We form a kind of procession with Sister Bridget, who carries a bronze cross and briskly leads the way. The sisters follow in their sensible shoes. They walk with such abandon to that gravesite that I think: *These may just be the only truly free people in America.*

I remember something I once read in Thich Nhat Hanh's *The Five Remembrances*: "We are of a nature to die. There is no way to escape death. . . . Our actions are our only true belongings. . . . Our actions are the ground on which we stand."

I look at Sister Phyllis's simple silver coffin ready to enter the earth and at the sisters in their secondhand clothes from a recycle shop. They know the secret. *Our actions are our only true belongings.*

The week after I return home from the funeral, two stories in the *New York Times* catch my eye. One chronicles the fate of the once-prosperous Simmons Bedding Co., maker of the famous Beautyrest mattress. Simmons changed hands several times in recent decades, with each successive owner acquiring increasing amounts of debt. A thousand workers—a quarter of Simmons's workforce—lost their jobs. The current owners, Thomas H. Lee Partners of Boston, have brought the company to the brink of Chapter 11 bankruptcy. But not before they paid themselves hundreds of millions of dollars in special dividends and fees. the *Times* calls what happened to Simmons "a tale of these financial times."

The second article was an obituary of financier Bruce Wasserstein, whom I remembered from my days at the *Wall Street Journal*. Wasserstein had engineered the kind of corporate takeovers that made billionaires of investment bankers while costing thousands of workers their livelihoods. He had died suddenly at the age of sixty-one, apparently of heart failure.

The sisters have a tradition whenever a community member dies. On the night before the funeral, they gather for storytelling. One of Sister Phyllis's cousins told of taking Sister Phyllis home for a visit. Sister Phyllis was particularly fond of the family's housekeeper. When it was time for her to return to the Mount, the cousin noticed Sister Phyllis wasn't wearing her coat. She had given it to the housekeeper.

"I said, 'Phyllis, didn't you say you just got that coat?'" the cousin recalled.

"That's okay," Sister Phyllis said. "I can get another one."

I thought of Sister Phyllis and Bruce Wasserstein and how they had come to the same end. I thought of the Simmons mattress company owners and how they—and all of us—are headed to that same end. Not a billion dollars or one cent can change that fact. And yet, it was Sister Phyllis—a woman who never had a personal bank account, who owned nothing except what she held in common with the community—who felt rich enough and secure enough to give away her only coat.

Sister Phyllis didn't know me. We never had a conversation. She was too ill for that by the time we met. But because of her, I know now that while dying is a painful process, it doesn't have to be lonely. We fear death because we don't know where it leads, just as we didn't know where we were headed when we made the journey from the womb into this life. But somehow we knew instinctively when it was time to forge ahead.

The theologian Karl Rahner has written, "The only thing that still counts at this stage is what we can take with us in death: that is, I myself as I was in the ultimate depths of my own heart, a heart that was either full of love or full of spite and hidden selfishness."

As much as Sister Phyllis taught me about death, she taught me even more about life. *Our actions are our only true belongings.* I like to think that because of Sister Phyllis, I wouldn't be afraid to give away my coat.

A Letter from France

I'm not someone who is prone to describing fortunate turns of events as "miracles." And yet, events keep happening that I never would have imagined. Call them "happenstance," "serendipity," "good fortune," or "dumb luck." Perhaps even call them "miracles." For some reason, they've occurred with greater frequency since I've been spending time at the Mount. I'll just call that *mystery*.

One evening, after I returned home from a two-week stay at the Mount, my husband handed me the pile of mail that had accumulated while I was gone. He pointed to an envelope with the distinctive blue slash marks of international mail. I glanced at it quickly, thinking it was probably from friends in the Czech Republic whom I've known since my days as a foreign correspondent. When I looked closer, I saw the return address said *Paris*. The letter inside drew me into a part of the past that lay forgotten for nearly twenty years.

In my junior year in college, I studied for a semester at the Sorbonne. It was the pivotal experience of my young life. I was a gawky nineteen-year-old from blue-collar Hudson County, New Jersey, with grandiose visions of my own sophistication. I soon met a young French woman two years older than me. Annick epitomized the kind of personal transformation I'd hoped my French sojourn magically would evoke. She was stylish, well traveled, and—most importantly perhaps— completely at ease around the opposite sex. We became as close as sisters. Her parents treated me like a second daughter. Maman Bracque, as I called Annick's mother, framed every silly poem I wrote about Paris in my imperfect French. Annick's father, whom I called Papa Romain, was a champion talker and storyteller who'd grown up in Marseille.

The Bracques worked as concierges in a turn-of-the-century apartment building, steps from the Eiffel Tower. It was a fashionable address, but as the concierges, they lived in a tiny apartment that doubled as the mail room for the building's well-to-do *locataires*. Despite the cramped quarters, their dinner table often was crowded with *les invites*. As a young woman, Maman Bracque had apprenticed in a restaurant and was a first-class cook. Her six-course meals were served on the good china, with every plate going back to the kitchen to be washed before the next course. My fondness for entertaining stems from the memory of those long, loving meals of *coq au roux* or *lapin a la Normande*, with much Beaujolais and laughter around the Bracques's dining room table. To this day, they remain my gold standard of hospitality.

When Annick's second child, Vincent, was born, she asked me to be his godmother. We kept in touch for several years afterward, and I returned frequently for visits to Paris. Here, our story takes a sadder turn.

Annick's path had led her to marriage and family life. I pursued a career in journalism, taking me to different locations. My high-energy career didn't leave me much time to foster personal relationships. But it was also true that at that point in my life, I just wasn't meeting men who were more interesting than my work. When I was thirty-five and still unmarried, my mother began getting desperate in my stead. Never mind that I was then writing for the largest newspaper in America, earning a good salary, living in a high-rise on Chicago's Lake Shore Drive, and had been a finalist for the Pulitzer Prize. In my mother's eyes, I wasn't "settled down." At one point, she had my sister-in-law show me a news item that said women over forty had a greater chance of being hijacked on an airplane than getting married.

Around this time, I spent a holiday with Annick and her family in France. My single status became Topic A for discussion with them too. Annick seemed to swing between envy that I could do as I pleased as a single woman and pity that I still hadn't found a mate. Her sentences often began with *"Toi, tu es seule, c'est domage que . . ."* ("You, you are alone, it's too bad that . . ."). Her husband's comments followed suit. I sensed my friends (like my poor mother) were beginning to believe I was somehow irrevocably defective.

I was so offended after that visit that I simply stopped writing to my friends. I severed a fifteen-year friendship because of a bruised ego. After a time, they stopped writing too.

Things might have stayed that way forever if that envelope hadn't arrived. Annick's letter began, "I hope you have not forgotten me and that you have kept the good memories of our youth." She went on to say that she had asked her daughter, now twenty-six, to search my name on the Internet. They knew about the broadcast work I was currently doing with PBS and about the poetry books I'd written. Annick said she and her husband had even tried to find my name in the telephone book on a trip they'd taken to New York. But the lines that caught in my throat were these: *Vincent has always regretted knowing so little of his American godmother.*

Focused on my wounded pride, I had not considered Vincent. I thought about all the birthdays, graduations, and Christmases we could have shared. I had not seen him since he was three or four. He was now twenty-four years old and engaged to be married!

I knew I couldn't resurrect the past, but I did have some measure of control over actions in the present. What had Thich Nhat Hanh written? *Our actions are our only true belongings. . . . Our actions are the ground on which we stand.*

A few days later, when I could collect my thoughts, I telephoned my long-lost friends. We reconnected as if no time had passed at all. A few months later, my husband and I spent a week with them in Paris. We were able to celebrate Vincent's twenty-fifth birthday together. Papa Romain had passed away, but Maman Bracque was as warm and kindhearted as ever. She knitted slippers for my husband and me and sent us home with handmade scarves for my stepdaughters and toys for Charley's granddaughter. Like the father in the parable of the prodigal son, she embraced me as if I were a daughter come back to life. Not only had my friends not stopped looking for me, they had never stopped loving me.

In hindsight, my own ultrasensitivity led to the rupture in our friendship. My penance for that is the years we lost between us. I can only go forward now, vowing to never let something like that happen again. That is my *conversatio* in all this.

I honestly don't think I would have reunited with my friends if they hadn't reached out to me first. The experience taught me something quite valuable. We can set a course to work on some aspect of *conversatio*, such as trying to be more patient, more humble, less volatile. But sometimes, when we're lucky, *conversatio* simply arrives. It comes through others . . . as a gift.

Winemaking

For nearly three years now, I have been coming to this monastery. With any luck, some infinitesimal stem cells of *conversatio* have been dividing and multiplying inside of me to make me a more compassionate, more humble, more *human* human being.

With summer's end, the grapevines enter into their fullness. As I look forward to the transformation that lies ahead for the fruit, I await with equal anticipation the inner transformation that may yet show itself in me. On a sizzling afternoon in late August, Sister Judith Sutera and I set out one last time for the vineyard. Its fruit has grown into plump, inverted pyramids of purple and yellow. It is time for winemaking.

"How can I be sure I'm picking ripe ones?" I ask her.

"If they're not ripe, they look like these," she says, cupping a handful of grapes that are an opaque yellow-green. "The ripe ones are translucent; the light goes right through them." I suppose you can say the same about the most spiritually mature people. They're also the most transparent. I think of Sister Lillian, Sister Kathleen, Sister Thomasita, and so many of the sisters who seem unafraid to be who they are. *The light goes right through them.*

Our tools are basic: a crate, a bucket, and a towel. The ingredients are simple, too: grapes, water, sugar, and air.

We don white aprons. The grapes are moist and sticky as we pluck them one by one from their stems or in clusters of twos and threes and toss them in the bucket. It is tedious, repetitive work. My lower back begins to ache. I remember the California grape pickers I saw on television in my childhood, their weathered, dignified faces. They were seeking not just better wages but the right to take more bathroom breaks and to stop for drinks of water. If my back aches after just a half hour, I wonder how those workers spent hours bent over fields in scorching heat. "Stoop labor," they called it. Our wine isn't for the dinner table; it's for the Eucharist at next year's Holy Thursday Mass. I smile, thinking of the people who will, one by one, step up to the altar and sip "our" wine from a communion cup.

The main event of winemaking is, of course, the crushing of the grapes. We have joked all day about whether I am going to "dance," that is, smash the grapes with my feet. I opt for using my hands. I thrust my fingers into the bucket and begin pressing. It is like squeezing several soft, cool, tiny balls—rather therapeutic.

The aroma of the crushed grapes is something unique—what I imagine the color green would smell like if green had a scent. We add a few large pitchers of water to the bucket. Then we each dip a forefinger into the liquid and touch it to our tongues. At the moment, our wine tastes more like Welch's grape juice.

The pulp stains my fingertips green and lodges beneath my fingernails. We place a hand towel over each bucket and secure them with large rubber bands. I'm ready to add the sugar and pour the juice into the one-gallon bottles we've washed out, but Sister Judith tells me it's too soon for that. The juice needs to set for three to five days. Winemaking, I am beginning to see, is also a lesson in patience.

"I've always said you can't fully understand the Eucharist if you don't have experience with the actual elements of the Eucharist," Sister Judith says. "It's interesting that Jesus chose bread and wine. They're two things that once changed can't revert to their original form. You can remove the lettuce from a salad, and it's still lettuce. But bread can't go back to being grain, and wine can't return to the grapes. It's a total transformation. And in each case, there's an agent. Yeast in the case of bread, sugar in the case of wine. In the Eucharist, I think that agent is the Spirit."

Yes, I think, *Jesus the poet, the dramatist, the connoisseur of metaphor.*

Like grade school kids growing potatoes in paper cups, Sister Judith and I can't wait to check the contents of our buckets the following day. Our wine has spent the night cooling in the basement. We remove the towel from one of the buckets as if we were lifting a coffin cover. The grape skins have risen to the surface and have turned a putrid brown color that makes me think of decomposing flesh. The juice smells like rot too. We dip a ladle beneath the scrim of grape skins and take a sip. Surprisingly, the juice tastes a lot better than it looks. And yes, it's becoming wine.

We amuse ourselves for the next several minutes conjuring up all the winemaking metaphors we can think of. The grapes must be crushed to become something even more valuable (wisdom through suffering). The skins decompose like a body, and what is left emerges as something wholly new (death to new life). The juice must sit undisturbed for several days (value in stillness).

We have taken only a sip of what is turning into wine, and yet we have become drunk on metaphor. But Sister Judith was right. Jesus knew what he was communicating when he promised to remain present in the bread and the wine, these most basic of table staples. Now when I take the communion cup, I think of the fruit's long journey from the vine to the altar table. Winemaking is its own form of *conversatio*, the conversion of one substance into something totally new. Without words, the grapevines instruct me. This time, I listen.

Acceptance

When I return to the Mount, it is late autumn. The season has been benevolently mild, as if the year had decided to offer up a parting gift. The warm spell ended today, as we knew it one day would. On a morning of blustery wind and rain, I drive about twenty-five miles south to Leavenworth, Kansas, to visit Father Owen Purcell, the retired abbot from St. Benedict's Abbey who works as a chaplain at both St. Mary's University and the famous federal prison there. Abbot Owen once told me that his tries to live "in the continuous mystery of now."

Route 73 South winds around farm fields that swell and loll. A convention of sparrows, more than I've ever seen together at one time, course through the sky like long brown scarves. They swoop toward the fields and then fly up again, repeatedly. Why they do this is a mystery of nature understood perhaps by birds alone.

I never know what topic will be on the abbot's mind. By whatever stroke of luck or marvel, it usually ends up being the very thing I need to hear to get me through whatever conflict, confusion, or indecision I am experiencing at the time.

Recently, he has been rereading the personal journals of Thomas Merton. He opens to a passage Merton wrote on March 2, 1966, and reads it to me:

> "A flash of sanity: the momentary realization that there is *no need* to come to certain conclusions about persons, events, conflicts, trends, even trends toward evil and disaster. . . .What do such judgments mean? Little or nothing. Things are as they are in an immense whole of which I am a part and which I cannot pretend to grasp . . . moving where

movement is possible and keeping still when movement is unnecessary, realizing that things will continue to define themselves and will be more clear to me if I am silent, attentive, obedient to [God's] will. . . .

Things are as they are in an immense whole of which I am a part and which I cannot pretend to grasp. I've been fortunate enough to experience many occasions when I felt a part of something larger than myself, that "immense whole" of which Merton writes. But to acknowledge that I can't grasp the meaning of every incident in my life is more of a struggle. I want to, I *need* to figure out the reasons for everything. Why is my producer so fixated on controlling things? Why won't my stepdaughters accept me? Why do I behave so badly when I think I'm not "liked"?

But Benedictine spirituality allows for a healthy dose of mystery. And that means accepting myself where I am, even when I can't figure out how I got there. It's a far cry from how I've always viewed my career: an ascent measured in achievements and salary increases. In the Benedictine worldview, success lies in the process, the small steps of becoming. I don't have to worry about whether I'm going to one day have my own radio show or write a bestseller. I am where I am now, and this very moment in my life is rich unto itself. As Merton suggests, "things will continue to define themselves and will be more clear" the more I am still, silent, and attentive. If only I could learn to believe that, live that.

Over his long years as a spiritual director, Abbot Owen has collected a wide array of counseling tools. He opens a thick volume with a black leather cover, and says he has been rereading one passage in particular, taking its advice to heart. He asks me to read it aloud:

> And acceptance is the answer to all my problems today. When I am disturbed, it is because I find some person, place, thing, or situation—some fact of my life—unacceptable to me, and I can find no serenity until I can accept that person, place, thing, or situation as being exactly the way it is supposed to be at this moment. Nothing, absolutely nothing, happens in God's creation by mistake. . . . I need to concentrate not so much on what needs to be changed in the world, as to what needs to be changed in me and my attitudes.

I am sure Abbot Owen can hardly imagine the emotions these words whip up as I face another Christmastime visit with my stepdaughters.

Christmas, Conversatio, *and a Roll of Salami*

Before heading off to my stepdaughter's home, I return for a second Christmas at the Mount, wondering if it can possibly top last year's experience. Snow falls heavily on Christmas Eve. Abbot Owen has come over from the abbey and moved into the guest quarters at the Mount so that the sisters will be sure to have a celebrant for Christmas Eve Mass. Holed up indoors, the guests become an ad hoc family with Abbot Owen as the kindly grandfather to us all. I notice, though, that he participates in the camaraderie only to a point, then he excuses himself and retires, with a book or his thoughts, to his room. He tells me later, "I can only take so much chitchat."

At one point, I find myself alone in the lounge. I slump into one of the rocking chairs. For once, no guests are bustling in and out of their rooms. No cars start up in the parking lot or crackle along the driveway. Even the usual thrum of machinery at the Midwest Grain Products plant has fallen silent. I look out the window on this gray shroud of a day. What a rare and precious thing it is to sit absolutely still in complete silence. I think of the visit my husband Charley and I will make after Christmas to my stepdaughter's home. The grandbaby will be there, and so will Charley's son-in-law, of course. My younger stepdaughter and her boyfriend will be there too—the first time we will all be together at Christmas.

In the stillness of that moment, I realize I don't feel so angry anymore at my stepdaughters for all the past hurts and disagreements. Looking at the situation from their perspective, I see two young women who had a stable home with two parents and one day woke to find it would never be that way again. Then, just as they were beginning to forge a new relationship with each of their parents separately, I entered the picture. Now, there is a third person to relate to, someone they don't know well and didn't ask to have in their lives.

I would like to tell my stepdaughters that I understand how they feel, that I'm sorry they lost the family life they once knew, and that we can try to forge a new family together—not better than what they had but still worthwhile. I am sorry about the rocky start we've had. I know it has not been easy for them and that I have not always been patient. I think about writing them a letter or a note.

Maybe this too is *conversatio*: the hope hidden in things as they are. I sit silently for about a half hour. When I rise from my chair, I feel as if I've rested for hours. *Sleep in heavenly peace.*

Abbot Owen celebrates Christmas Eve Mass in liturgical vestments and tennis shoes. "Only those with a joyful heart will appreciate the irony, the incongruity of the Christmas story," he says. "Think of Julian of Norwich. All will be well. All will be well. You've got to be kidding me! But in the final analysis, *all will be well* because of Christmas. At Christmas, love itself spills over because that is the nature of our God."

A typical Abbot Owen homily. Simple, insightful.

When my husband arrives at the Mount the day after Christmas, the roads are still treacherous. He makes it all the way from Illinois without incident until the Mount's driveway. He ditches the car a few yards from the guesthouse, then walks to the door in drifts three feet high. When he tells the two sisters who let him in that his car is stuck, they say in unison, "Call, Elaine!" They mean Sister Elaine Fischer, the director of maintenance.

Within minutes, we hear the growl of a snowplow outside our window. Perched on top like a tank commander is Sister Elaine, who is ensconced in an all-weather suit. She hops off the plow, slides handily under the car, and hooks a chain around its fender for the tow.

Safely inside again, we exchange gifts with the sisters. Sister Anne, the prioress, presents me with a construction paper Christmas tree bearing the signatures of each of the Mount sisters. Even the elderly, infirm sisters in the assisted care unit have written their names on it, which touches me deeply. Sister Thomasita gives me a woven prayer rug from her visit to a Tibetan school in India.

The day after Christmas is a Sunday, and we gather again for Mass. It is also the Feast of St. Stephen, who was stoned to death, the first Christian martyr. In his homily, Abbot Owen notes the marked difference between the readings on Christmas and today: "Yesterday, it was all birth and light and rejoicing and peace. Today, it's dissent and violence and blood on the ground." Stephen tried to preach the Gospel, but the people chose to cover their ears rather than listen. "If someone approaches us to speak to us today, will we respond by covering our ears?" the abbot asks. As he finishes the homily, I look up at the chapel's blue windows. For the first time in two days, sun streams through the stained glass, like a river of gold.

❧

Charley and I leave the Mount with the usual sense of sadness. But for once, I am actually looking forward to being with my stepdaughters and Charley's granddaughter, who is old enough now to delight in the holiday as only children can.

As we head out, Sister Judith presents us with an emergency travel kit in the form of a World War II–vintage suitcase that probably belonged to some young novice. She has packed it with hand warmers, a red flag, a candle, matches, a bottle of water, and a package of kitty litter in case we get stuck on ice. It is the Mount's hospitality extended to our journey beyond.

About two hours into our drive, my husband's cell phone rings. It is my older stepdaughter calling. A wrinkle has developed in the plan for our visit. My husband's ex-wife was supposed to have departed a few days before our arrival, but she is still at my stepdaughter's house, occupying the only guest bedroom. She has a cold and can't travel. The thought of my husband's ex-wife looming over our visit like the Ghost of Christmases Past hardly fills me with cheer. My stepdaughter says we're still welcome to come if we like. She assures us her mother is confined to her bed in the guest room. She says we can sleep on a blow-up mattress in the basement. She adds that my younger stepdaughter and her boyfriend are also sleeping in the basement, on a futon. "I suppose we'll form a cozy foursome down there," I snarl at my husband after he hangs up. I reject the suggested sleeping arrangement as ludicrous.

If I were a more humorous person, a little less hot-tempered, a little less Sicilian, I might find this turn of events comical. Instead, I'm livid. I can't understand why my stepdaughter waited until we were halfway to her house before springing this news. I suggest that we turn around for home and tell her we'll visit another time, but my husband insists we forge on. These are *his* days to spend with his two daughters, by gosh, and he's not going to allow his ex-wife's presence force him to miss them.

We finally reach a compromise. We'll go to my stepdaughter's, but we won't stay at the house. We'll go to a hotel. We won't sleep in the basement alongside my stepdaughter and her boyfriend.

When we arrive, my husband's ex-wife isn't out of sight under the covers of her sick bed. In fact, she is walking across the living room, big as life, carrying a cup of tea. Without acknowledging us, she proceeds to the guest bedroom. Everyone behaves as if all this is perfectly natural. We exchange hellos and hugs with my stepdaughters, and my husband and I lift our giggling granddaughter in the air. So far so good, I guess.

While we're having dinner, the cell phone rings again. It is the dog sitter who is caring for our two dachshunds, one of whom is sick. We both rise from the table to take the call, leaving our half-eaten dinners. When we return, the table has been cleared. "Guess dinner is over," I whisper to my husband, trying to not feel irked.

We move into the living room to exchange gifts. Each year, my husband receives a list from my stepdaughters of what they would like as presents. Usually, they are rather large and expensive gifts. I think of gifts as something freely offered, freely received. And every year, my husband reminds me that not everyone thinks like me.

From my younger stepdaughter and her boyfriend, I receive a wrapped cylindrical package. It is a roll of salami. A *small* roll of salami. *Okay*, I'm thinking, *they know I'm Italian American, so they must think I like salami.* (I hardly ever eat it, except in an antipasto salad.) *Don't be petty*, I tell myself, remembering the chapter on humility in *The Rule*. We move on to their next gift. It is a container of tea. I remind myself, *Okay, I drink tea.* The gift from my other stepdaughter is more tea. At this point, I wonder, *After four years of marriage, are the only things my stepdaughters know about me that I'm Italian American and like to drink tea?*

My husband opens his gifts: a DVD of a movie we've already seen and some silly action flick. By now, I'm thinking, *To hell with humility. Can't they get him something better than discount DVDs?* He does, however, get a nice set of audiotapes of poets reading their work from my younger stepdaughter. She notes when he opens the gift that she thought it was something we both would enjoy. But I'm still focused on that roll of salami.

My mood takes an appreciable turn and not in the direction of merriment. I'm fairly certain people sense that I'm upset, but I doubt they know why.

When we get to the hotel, I blow up about the Christmas presents. Normally, I'm grateful for even the smallest gift. I'm certain that if one of the Mount sisters had given me a roll of salami for Christmas, I'd rave about it and say it was the best darn roll of salami I'd ever tasted. So why did I feel humiliated when it came from one of my stepdaughters?

As the night goes on, I feel increasingly embarrassed by the way I acted. I wonder how I'll be able to face my stepdaughters the next day. Worse than the regret I'm feeling is the sense that I'm an utter failure at *conversatio.* I've known for a long time that one of my greatest challenges is my relationship with my stepdaughters. My husband has pleaded with me to keep working at it, for his sake. It is the right thing to do. I know it. And yet, I keep on falling. Abbot Owen was so right in his homily the day after Christmas. All too quickly peace and light give way to dissent and "blood on the ground."

A Walk in the Cemetery

Some of my most memorable conversations with the sisters have occurred during walks in the cemetery. On a mild winter day of glittering sun, Sister Thomasita and I stroll past the cemetery's stone Stations of the Cross. I confess to her my embarrassment over the way I reacted to my stepdaughters' Christmas gifts. The same questions confound me again: Why can't I live *conversatio* in my day-to-day life, and why can I write about humility but not live it? She listens intently but offers no answers. She promises to think about what I've told her. She says, "We'll talk again."

A few weeks later, I receive this e-mail:

I want to thank you for our walk in the cemetery the last time you were here. As we walked and you talked of your pain and your insights, I suddenly thought again of 1 Corinthians. "Love is patient, love is kind and not jealous; love does not brag and is not arrogant, does not act unbecomingly; it does not seek its own, is not provoked, does not take into account a wrong suffered, does not rejoice in unrighteousness, but rejoices with the truth, bears all things, believes all things, hopes all things, endures all things. Love never fails."

I recalled a retreat director challenging us to read the passage over slowly, deliberately, several times. . . . She suggested we reflect on the word "Love" and substitute the word "God" each time love is mentioned. Something happened inside me when I did that. Then, she challenged us to substitute our own name for the word "Love." Until the end of the retreat, we were to use our name in that way, slowly reflecting on the passage. I think of this often, and for some reason, I have been thinking of it ever since our walk.

I take up Sister Thomasita's suggestion . . . several times. It *is* a powerful experience to say to myself, "*Judy* is patient. *Judy* is kind and not jealous. *Judy* does not brag and is not arrogant. . . ." Soon I will have to face my stepdaughters again, and possibly even their mother. There are times I think I don't have the wherewithal even to be in the same the room with them. Then I reread 1 Corinthians. I know what I have to do. I have to keep on showing up for my stepdaughters. Then we will at least stand a chance of coming to know one another as we each are: full of gifts and full of flaws.

I think of what the Desert Fathers said of the spiritual life. We are always beginners. We fall and we rise, we fall and we rise. *Conversatio* means continuing to show up for life—even when we'd rather not, even when we think we can't.

Sister Thomasita once said something else to me about *conversatio*. "You are living *conversatio*," she said. "Your struggle, that's the *conversatio*." And that has given me hope, hope that I don't have to be at my best all the time. I just have to be human. *I fall and I rise, I fall and I rise.*

The Real Behind the Real

I had experienced the Mount in every season, spent Christmases and Easters there, and celebrated with sisters on their fiftieth and even seventy-fifth anniversaries in the community. One of the events I had yet to witness was a final profession of vows: the moment a woman makes a lifetime commitment to the monastic community. I felt it would be a fitting coda to my journey with the sisters.

On the Feast of the Epiphany, a slender, dark-haired woman knelt beneath a marble baldachin in St. Scholastica Chapel. She was there to answer a single question: "What do you seek?"

She responded, "I ask that I may follow Christ in the company of this community all the days of my life."

With these words, Sister Elizabeth Carrillo, thirty-eight years old, became the newest—and youngest—member of the Mount community. A talented vocalist and concert violinist, Sister Elizabeth could have chosen a different path. She didn't.

The day before her final vows, I spent a few hours talking with Sister Elizabeth. "Monastic life," she told me, "is a way of trying to cut through the superficial . . . a way to see through to the real behind what we think of as real."

On the surface, the details of Elizabeth Carrillo's life make her one of the most improbable candidates to walk through a monastery's doors. Most of her adult life she considered herself a "spiritual atheist."

Her path to the Benedictines was full of side alleys, meandering from medieval music to the Psalms to Orthodox chant and the writings of Thomas Merton. Finally, it led her to this place. Yet, in hindsight, her arrival at Mount St. Scholastica seems to have been all but predestined.

Along her journey, she stumbled on *The Rule of St. Benedict*. "It was a musty old copy from the library. There was something about it. I didn't know much about monasticism at the time. So it was a revelation that this book is still a living, breathing inspiration for people. It's not just some relic from late antiquity. That sort of started things for me."

Then she purchased her first Bible. She says, "It felt like I was doing something so naughty, like buying pornography." Fearing her family's ridicule, she kept her religious yearnings a secret.

On a break from school, she visited a Greek Orthodox monastery. "That was my first Easter Vigil." She came away with a gift: a prayer book. It turned out to be the Liturgy of the Hours she would one day pray as a monastic sister.

After graduation, she taught music at a community college, played in an orchestra, and taught violin in her own studio. She dated a man for over a year, and they talked about marrying. Then, "I had this dream one night that we *had* married, that we had kids and had adopted kids. And I remember thinking in the dream, 'Does this mean I can't go to the monastery?'" Eventually, they broke up.

Trolling the Internet one day, she decided to type in the word *monastery*. "To this day, I don't know why I began looking for retreats at women's monasteries because that wasn't even on my radar. Within fifteen minutes of clicking on, I found the Mount in Kansas."

Sister Elizabeth applied to work that summer in the Mount's music conservatory with Sister Joachim Holthaus, one of its resident composers.

"I fell in love with the liturgy right from the start. Back when I was in college, the first scripture I read was the Psalms. I didn't realize back then that I was already doing *lectio*. When I'd read a Psalm, I'd wait and pause. It would take me a long time to get through one. It wasn't until I had the experience of praying with the community that I realized this is how they do it. The fact that the Psalms are the core to the liturgical prayers we do was like coming home."

For those who seek to spend their lives in a monastic community, the path to commitment is a slow, arduous, intentional walk. All in all, it is like having an engagement period of no fewer than five years. Perhaps it's the reason most of the people who make it to final vows end up staying a lifetime, while 50 percent of the people who exchange marriage vows don't.

On the night before Sister Elizabeth's final profession, the Mount community gathers for Vespers in the choir chapel. Sister Elizabeth walks alone to the altar and kneels facing the community. One by one, the sisters lay their hands on her head and offer a spoken or silent blessing.

On the day of the profession, the sisters march two by two into St. Scholastica Chapel. In a gesture that unites them with Benedictines throughout the centuries, they bow before the altar and then to one another. A tall white candle burns in the center aisle.

Sister Elizabeth enters last, carrying the paper on which she has written, by hand, her vows.

She stands facing the altar, her arms spread wide, and sings three times, "Receive me, O Lord, as you have promised, that I may live. Disappoint me not in my hope."

She later told me that one of the most dramatic moments for her was when she lay face down on the floor of the sanctuary, covered by a funeral pall—dying to an old way of life and being reborn to a new way of living. In that moment, she says, she gave her life over to "the radical unknown."

"Benedict asks, 'Is there anyone here who yearns for life and desires to see good days?' We've been told the good life is what the world tells us it is. So people are seeing this shiny bauble and think this is what they need to put their energy into instead of what really is the good life," Sister Elizabeth explains.

Describing the qualities it takes to be a monk, the Trappist writer Matthew Kelty once said, "We like it if you notice rain, feel the wind, hear the birds, smell the soup. We like you to be aware, not asleep; alive, not dead; in touch, not gone." I think that is the "good life" Sister Elizabeth discovered at the Mount. It is probably what I had been searching for when I first began my visits to the monastery, though I could not articulate it then. It is what I take away now.

VII.

The Monastery of the Heart

THE ABBOT AND THE RABBI

The abbot of a large monastery was troubled by the amount of discord and grumbling that existed among the monks of his abbey. He tried cajoling, teaching, and censuring, but nothing seemed to alter the bickering.

Finally the abbot heard of a rabbi living in a nearby town. This rabbi was renowned for his great wisdom and the abbot went to seek his counsel.

After hearing the abbot's story, the rabbi sat silently and very still for a long while.

Then he said to the abbot, "Go and tell your monks you have received this prophecy: "The Messiah is among you."

The abbot returned to his abbey and told his monks of the word he had received. Each one, knowing his sinful nature, began to wonder in turn, "Surely it is not I, the Messiah."

They pondered silently who it could be. Some monks wondered, "Perhaps it is Brother Paul, he often cares for the sick." Or, "Perhaps it is Father Luke, who helps the younger monks carry their loads."

From that day forward, peace returned to the monastery. Stories of the monks' kindness reached far beyond the monastery's walls. Young men came in great numbers to join the community, and many pilgrims came to pray there. All were reminded of what the abbot had once been told: "The Messiah is among you."

—Wisdom Story
told by Sister Lillian Harrington, "Pilgrim Minister"

What, then, can be made of this journey?

I wish I could say my visits to the Mount miraculously tamed my bad temper or healed my relationship with my stepdaughters. But that would not be *conversatio*. *Conversatio* isn't a sudden tectonic shift. It is more like the steady etching of water on a shoreline. It is the work of everyday life.

And yet, I *have* changed, if only in infinitesimal ways. When I first met Sister Thomasita, I was struck by her stillness, not only the quietness of her voice but even her movements. I used to think some people were just naturally quiet. I know now that you can cultivate that kind of stillness. I find I am a quieter person in both the way I speak and in the amount I speak. Periodically throughout my day, I catch bite-size interludes of silence, as my schedule doesn't allow for regularly carved-out periods of calmness and quiet.

For most of my career, I thought of success as a moving target. Every new achievement, whether a bigger job at a more prestigious newspaper or the publication of another book, seemed like a goalpost that faded quickly into the rearview mirror as I sped on to the next challenge. But my time at the Mount changed the way I think about success. There are still many goals I've set for myself that I haven't achieved. (I'd love to host a radio program on the religion factor in breaking news, for instance.) But from the Benedictines, I've learned to appreciate where I am in any given moment. It is enough to simply live my life and love the people I love.

I can't say I'm reconciled totally with the fact of death, but the examples that Sister Mary Noel and Sister Phyllis gave by their deaths have removed some of the terror. I think often of what Sister Mary Noel said about embracing the fullness of life so that when death comes, I can be ripe as that autumn leaf, ready to let go. For now, I consider my life still a work in progress. If at this moment I had to answer those billboard ads that ask *Where will you spend eternity?*, I'd probably have to say, "Purgatory."

As for my temper, it still erupts too often. But lately I find myself pausing a little longer before the fuse gets lit. Before I open my mouth, I apply Sister Micaela's standard: Is what I am about to say true? Is it kind? Is it necessary? One great sadness remains my relationship with stepdaughters. But attending my younger stepdaughter's wedding recently, I gained a certain insight. A number of guests stood up and praised her compassion for others, her thoughtfulness. I wondered if I don't see that side of my stepdaughter's character because I'm not looking for it. I remembered a passage Abbot Owen had shared with me: "I need to concentrate not so much on what needs to be changed in the world, as to what needs to be changed in me and my attitudes."

"I am rowing," Anne Sexton wrote in one of her best poems. "I am rowing / though the oar locks stick and are rusty . . . / though the wind pushes me back / and I know that island will not be perfect." And as fine as it is to reach our destination, we know from Odysseus and all the great heroes of myth that it is the journey that matters most. It is only when we put down our oars and stop moving forward that we grow feeble and die.

I used to think of monasteries as hopeless throwbacks to the past, a case of "let the last sister standing turn out the lights." Now I see them as windows to the future, a future we desperately need in our society—one that stresses consensus over competition, simplicity over consumption, service over self-aggrandizement, quietude over constant chatter, community over individual gain. There will always be a place for monasteries, Thomas Merton once said, because the world will always need "signs of contradiction."

The past few decades have been dominated by technology innovators who built better, faster systems of information delivery. But information isn't wisdom. Every age needs meaning makers. Meaning makers point us to what C. S. Lewis called the *real* real world. That's what the Benedictines have been doing for more than 1,500 years. As the MasterCard ad says, "Priceless."

There is, of course, a danger in perpetuating a myth of monastic life. Did I ever see negative things in my time at the monastery? Yes, of course. I once (once!) saw a tired sister get testy with another sister. I saw the prioress lose her temper, then apologize a short time later. There was occasional gossip, but it didn't hold a candle to the gossiping and backbiting I experienced in the newsrooms where I worked. No one sugarcoated the sacrifices monastic life requires. Abbot Owen wasn't afraid to admit nights are often long and lonely. And despite the substantial support the sisters enjoy from their community members, in a whimsical moment, Sister Chris once confided that she sometimes misses being the jewel in just one other person's eyes. Nor is the monastery a setting from which to flee from the world. It has, as Sexton puts it in her poem, "the flaws of life, the absurdities of the dinner table." What you find there, though, is a space for joining hands with others, where listening and transformation can occur. It is a place, as Thomas Merton put it, for "wrestling with the angel."

In many ways, I feel as if my entire past led me to this monastery on a hill. I arrived with a basketful of questions. I left with far more than I had sought. The sisters like to say that anyone who spends a measure of time at the Mount becomes just as much a part of it as its distinctive blue windows. You come here, and you fall in love . . . with the setting . . . with the prayer life . . . with the community. You can leave Mount St. Scholastica, but it never leaves you.

On the eve of taking her final vows, Sister Elizabeth Carrillo had told me, "If you take the time to know yourself, you go beyond your own personal understanding into a universal understanding of humanity. You arrive at a point where you are no longer going inward, but knowledge begins to shoot outward. It isn't just a knowledge of things. It's a wisdom that comes to us through the Spirit."

Through that wisdom of the Spirit I carry the Mount with me wherever I go. I always sensed whenever I visited the Mount that I was crossing into a deeper reality. I still think it's easier to enter that reality if you reside within the monastery's walls, but I now believe in something else, too. "The real cloister or enclosure is the heart," the Cistercian Abbess Gail Fitzpatrick has written. I believe in a monastery of the heart. That is what I hope I have been building. This story ends with me still building.

Postscript

Even in a place that puts a premium on stability, changes do occur. And several have taken place since I made my first journey to the Mount. The Broken Spoke Café on Route 59 went out of business, so you'll be out of luck if you try to stop there for the sausage scrapple. Midwest Grain Products tore down a portion of its plant, but is still a watchful presence in the center of Atchison. The Cowboy Cobbler and most of the other small businesses along Route 59 were washed out in the summer floods of 2011. A new four-lane concrete bridge is rising over the Missouri River to replace the "structurally deficient" Amelia Earhart Bridge.

Sister Mary Elizabeth Schweiger, who sought to be a "non-anxious presence" within the monastery, stepped down after thirteen years as subprioress and is on a long sabbatical. Mary Cummings, Sister Lillian Harrington's older sister, passed away peacefully on Thanksgiving Day 2011, "bringing gratitude for the gift of her long and full life to God, the Giver of all gifts," as Sister Thomasita described it. Mary was 104. Sister Lillian was at her bedside when she died. At age ninety-six, Sister Kathleen Egan now ranks as the oldest member of the Mount community. She cherishes each new day and is still fervently nonviolent.

Acknowledgments

Grateful acknowledgment is extended to Jim Manney, Tom Artz, and Margaret Lewis, who read early drafts of this manuscript; to Lisa Breger, Annie Parker, and Dick Homan, who offered invaluable feedback throughout the writing; to the "Valente committee" at the Mount—Sisters Susan Holmes, Joan Offenberger, Deborah Peters, and Mary Teresa Morris—who helped with accuracy; to Sister Thomasita Homan, who introduced me to the Mount community and became my trusted guide; to Sister Anne Shepard, prioress, and Sister Mary Elizabeth Schweiger, subprioress, who gave me unprecedented access to the life of the community; to Ray Clem of Atchison, for providing me with all those lucky Kennedy half-dollar coins; to my agent, Michele Rubin of The Writers House in New York, for her unflagging faith in this book and to her helpful staff; to Lil Copan of Sorin Books, for her masterful editing; and to my husband, Charles Reynard, who is my companion in writing and life, my best editor and best friend.

Appendix

The Benedictine Sisters of Mount St. Scholastica

Sienna Rohlfer, Lillian Harrington, Helen Buening, Devota Klamet, Ann Zager, Brendan Fry, Loretta Schirmer, Kathleen Egan, Sharon Holthaus, Paula Howard, Joachim Holthaus, Cyprian Vondras, Mary Ethel Burley, Benedicta Boland, Gertrude Nagel, Laura Haug, Marjorie McGrath+, Norma Honz, Joyce Meyers, Rosina Baumgartner, Irmina Miller, Mary Kathryn Taylor, Philomene Glotzbach, Marie Louise Krenner, Mary Margaret Bunck, Seraphine Tucker, Celinda Medina, Loretta Wiesner, Mary Blaise Cillessen, Mauricita Schieber, Roberta Schachle, Frances Yarc, Mary Owen Leutloff, Elaine Gregory, Mary Benet Obear, Mary Cecile Ihle, Laetitia Chavez, Brigid Kelliher+, Evelyn Gregory, Joan Taylor, Eunice Ballmann, Florentine Motichek, Miriam Schnoebelen, Mary Mel L'Ecuyer, Bettina Tobin, DeMontfort Knightley, Jeremy Dempsey, Johnette Putnam, Dorothy Heideman, Margaret Ann LaCapra, Alice Brentano, Noreen Hurter, Gabrielle Kocour, Marie Ballmann, Maria Larkin, Rosemary Bertels, Mary Rae Schrick, Agnes Honz, Mary Benedict Jacobs, Bernelda Nanneman, Joan Offenburger, Lucille Borengasser, Amelia Nowatzke, Mary Ann Fessler, Mary Lucy Kramer, Mary Grace Malaney, Jan Futrell, Berlinda Gallegos, Mary Ellen Auffert, Sharon Murray, Trinitas Miles+, Rita Claire Judge, Mary Beth

Niehaus, Sheila Carroll, Thomasita Homan, Dorothy Wolters, Janelle Maes, Deborah Peters, Barbara Ann Mayer, Micaela Randolph, JoAnn Fellin, Elena Hernandez, Mary Irene Nowell, Mary Ann Dice, Mary Grosdidier, Mary Collins, Sylvia Kenkel, Delores Dolezal, Joanne Yankauskis, Eleanor Suther, Linda Zahner, Martha Schweiger, Genevieve Robinson, Jeannine Neavitt, Loretta McGuire, Mary Margaret Kean, Therese Elias, Ann Diettrich, Barbara McCracken, Angela Ostermann, Rosann Eckart, Fran Cross, Susan Holmes, Esther Fangman, Mary Elizabeth Schweiger, Cecilia Olson, Carol Ann Petersen, Maria Heppler, Alberta Hermann, Marilyn Schieber, Anne Shepard, Rita Killackey, Sharon Hamsa, Rose Marie Stallbaumer, Helen Mueting, Constance Krstolic, Mary Agnes Patterson, Judith Sutera, Marcia Ziska, Linda Herndon, Carolyn Rohde, Mary Teresa Morris, Chris Kean, Maria Nguyen, Patricia Seipel, Mary Rardin, Kathleen Flanagan, Eliene Goueva, Maria das Gracas Silva Morais, Susan Barber, Molly Brockwell, Bridget Dickason, Elaine Fischer, Lou Whipple, Diana Seago, Alice Smitherman, Mary Palarino, Barbara Conroy, Melissa Letts, Mary Kratina, Oanh Pham, Giselia Morais, Suzanne Fitzmaurice, Barbara Smith, Joselaine Ferreira, Elizabeth Carrillo, Ironide Nunes, Erica Seago, Jodi Hart.

Founded in 1865, Ave Maria Press,
a ministry of the Congregation of
Holy Cross, is a Catholic publishing
company that serves the spiritual and
formative needs of the Church and its
schools, institutions, and ministers;
Christian individuals and families; and
others seeking spiritual nourishment.

For a complete listing of titles from

Ave Maria Press

Sorin Books

Forest of Peace

Christian Classics

visit www.avemariapress.com

 ave maria press® / Notre Dame, IN 46556
A Ministry of the United States Province of Holy Cross